Hawk Job~
wc R appreciate
and admiration~
Rgds
Alan Mul

If Not Me, Then Who?

E. Cabell Brand explains with specific examples what he has learned in 85 years and how you can start now with local action to solve local, national, and global problems to help make the world a better and safer place for our children.

Commendations for:

If Not Me, Then Who?

Former Governor of Virginia Tim Kaine:

You are an inspiration. You have always looked at the world around you with a desire to use your gifts to serve others. And, your focused and energetic ministry to all—especially to the least of these—has improved the lives of thousands and thousands of people worldwide. I count it a blessing to know you. The book also makes clear that your spirit is still as strong as ever. Thanks for writing your story so that others can know just how much one person can do.

Tom Lovejoy, President of The Heinz Center:

This is a well-written and wonderfully inspiring book about a life of courage and vision and the joy of learning and making a difference in a changing world. A book for everyone.

Charles S. Robb former Governor of Virginia and US Senator:

There are those who "talk the talk", but don't "walk the walk"; and there are those who spend their lives helping others, yet are reluctant to proselytize. But to make a lasting difference in our communities, our country and our world, we need leaders who can do both. Cabell Brand has been leading by example for almost 70 years, and he's clearly not ready to slow down or rest on his laurels.

In his remarkable life story we learn how many different ways all of us could respond to the call to help meet the most basic challenges facing the human condition and spirit. By dedicating 20 percent of every week of his adult life to helping others (and occasionally scolding the rest of us for not doing more ourselves) he has made a real difference in the lives of countless thousands. Would that all who read his well-documented story of a life well lived could say the same.

Isabel Sawhill, Brookings Institution Senior Fellow:

What the world needs is more Cabell Brands who are not only dedicated to making the world a better place for the next generation but who are willing to commit the time and resources to making their ideals a reality. Imagine if everyone committed to spending 20 percent of their time giving back to the larger community? Imagine if everyone reached out to those less fortunate with concrete forms of help from early education to insuring children's health to assisting felons to successfully reenter the mainstream? Many people throw up their hands at the enormity of such tasks but I think, by thinking globally and acting locally, Cabell Brand has shown what can be accomplished by just one person. One thing leads to another so that working in partnership with others, one is able to greatly leverage one's own efforts. The "self-reinforcing cycle" then takes hold but only if someone primes the pump to get the whole process started, a process which Cabell Brand understands so well.

Gerald McCarthy, Executive Director,
Virginia Environmental Endowment:

Cabell Brand has written a hopeful and practical book for all those people who wish to live well, do well, and contribute to our shared human experience. With passion and practical wisdom, he has issued a clarion call to return to practicing the principles that since our republic's founding have made the United States a beacon of hope for the world and a land of opportunity for all. Commerce, conservation, and compassion combine in an extraordinary life and example for us all.

Mike Rosenzweig, Ph.D. Co-Founder, Seek
Education, Explore, DiScover (SEEDS), Director,
Virginia Tech Science Outreach Program:

Many books are being written about the subjects of Mr. Brand's book, but he has a lifetime of personal experiences to share that adds a pragmatic and sensible, and practical detention to some otherwise challenging subjects to deal with together. His thoughts are a "must read" for students studying environmental science, economics, political science, business, and any major/

minor in sustainable development. Anyone brave enough to be part of the changing world that is upon us now should read this book.

John B. Williamson, Chairman and CEO, RGC Resources:

Cabell Brand is living testament to the effectiveness of teaching and leading by example. His brief book provides convincing and inspirational evidence that a long term and disciplined personal commitment to thinking globally while acting locally can produce tangible and lasting results on issues that matter to society. His life story and personal success should inspire the young and old alike to understand they too can help make the world a more equitable and humane place through persistent involvement in local issues of importance and that access to opportunity is contingent on personal engagement.

Edward G. Murphy, M.D., President and CEO Carilion Clinic

I certainly agree that young people starting out in professional life would benefit from reading your book. However, I feel that the specific target audience is too limiting. I think your book has a message that would benefit all, regardless of age or career stage. It certainly spoke to me.

Davis Mastin, Chair, President's Circle of the National Academies and Distinguished Visiting Scholar, Media X at Stanford University:

Cabell Brand is someone few have heard of, but to those who have, he is often called an American hero. As impossible as it may seem for one person to do, Cabell has made a real difference locally on issues of poverty, economic opportunity, education, healthcare, environment, racial justice and peace. Each of these started with small local steps and often continued at the state, regional, national and international levels. Cabell tells these local stories in the simple language of young man from a small town in Virginia. But also he inspires the reader with glimpses of conversations like those with Nobel Prize winners Al Gore as they worked on the environment and Muhammad Yunus on poverty from the 1970s and '80s. He starts the book sharing a dinner party conversation with the US Shepherd Program for the Interdisciplinary Study of Poverty and Human Capability

Presidents, senators, congressmen, governors have spent and continue to spend the night at his home. But Cabell always ties it back to small local steps that if not taken, would have kept him from collaborations with such distinguished citizens of the world.

Cabell and his wife Shirley have lived extraordinary lives. Their work has helped tens of thousands of people live better lives.

This book inspired me. I am sure it will inspire many others.

Neil Rolde, Author and Former Legislator, York, Maine:

Cabell Brand has a lot to tell young Americans. This octogenarian Virginia gentleman has made a great financial success of his life, parlaying a small shoe-selling company into a major business that he later sold. But the point of his book is that his real success is not in what he took from the *economy*, but in what he gave back to the *community* – and, in this case, not simply the Western Virginia area where he lives, but the entire U.S. and, for that matter, our planet as a whole. Indeed, he begins his story at a private dinner with President Bill Clinton where he informed him about Community Service Block grants about to be cut and managed to have these potentially devastating blows to the poverty safety net rescinded. Cabell Brand, businessman and patriot par excellence, never forgot and still never forgets America's duty to its society as a whole. His book is a perfect lesson plan for new generations.

David Paylor, Director, Virginia Department of Environmental Quality:

Cabell Brand has laid out a clear example of servant leadership on behalf of current and future generations. As we continue to increase our numbers, we demand more and more of our limited resources and place our future in jeopardy. Cabell draws attention to a number of critical concerns and demonstrates how each of us, on behalf of our communities and the world, can and must become involved if we are to maintain productive lifestyles and a healthy planet. I encourage others to be encouraged by and follow his example.

Gerald Paul, Businessman and Instructor at Purdue University:

The title to Cabell Brand's book is arousing interest but most of all presents a compelling story of a man who has achieved a diverse variety of accomplishments. The book has one overriding quality – namely to make this world be a better place to live and grow up in. Here is a story of a man and his multiplicity of achievements that make me feel introspective. I hope that people who read this story will be energized to become the "Who" and do more to improve the lives of people around us – improve the quality of life in our country but starting with their local contacts and conditions.

Hunter D. Smith, Recent University of Virginia MBA Graduate:

While I have never been to a war zone and I hope I never will, I can only imagine the impact of seeing war-torn Germany and then witnessing the benefits of the Marshall Plan. I hope that others who read the book come away with the perspective of our universal connectivity and the global positive impact of a hand-up. The environment, the economy, and society's well-being are all related. Like Cabell and Jonathan Daniels, people need to define themselves as part of the whole and then make a conscious effort to think universally rather than selfishly.

If Not Me, Then Who?

*How you can help with Poverty, Economic
Opportunity, Education, Healthcare, Environment,
Racial Justice, and Peace Issues in America*

By: E. Cabell Brand, with Tommy Denton

iUniverse, Inc.
New York Bloomington

Dedication

This book is about the future — of our country, our planet and specifically of our grandchildren.

I would like to dedicate this book to my wife, Shirley, who was my partner along the way in each of my projects since our marriage. She has made it possible for me to undertake so many challenges and opportunities while she managed our growing family and guided us through a number of crises and tragedies. Her love and support remain the source of my blessing and joy.

Annual Summer Fun Fest with our children, spouses and 13 grandchildren

My ultimate hope lies with our grandchildren and the abiding desire that each of them will work with you and your family to make the world a better place for everyone.

"I am only one, but I am one. I cannot do everything, but I can do something. And because I cannot do everything, I will not refuse to do the something that I can do. What I can do, I should do, and what I should do, by the grace of God, I will do."

— Everett Edward Hale
19th-century American writer

Table of Contents

Special Note from the Author Cabell Brand

This book is not a personal memoir. I have tried to identify 6 major problems America faces today, and hopefully how you, the reader, and all of us can help solve them.

In the years that I have been planning this book, I have learned that each phase of my life has been enriched by multi-dimensional experiences, each drawing depth, perspective and insight from the others. Much has been said of the principle of thinking globally and acting locally. I have found this not only to be true, but with vision and determination, I realize that local successes may also release the forces of a perpetual cycle that in turn leads to improving global conditions.

I hope that those who read this book will come to appreciate, as I have, that each generation must contribute to our "more perfect union."

My ultimate goal is simple: To exhort by example and challenge the current generation to begin thinking, planning and organizing to create, sustain and strengthen the American society, with the equal opportunity we want and expect our children, and their children, to inherit.

Cabell Brand

Introduction

By: Dr. Harlan Beckley

Director, Shepherd Program on Poverty and Human Capability

I came to know Cabell Brand as an advocate and supporter of the Shepherd Program on Poverty and Human Capability, an educational innovation at Washington and Lee University. In the process of our collaboration, Cabell has also become my mentor and friend. Cabell's enormous contributions to the success of the Shepherd Program in the last decade are only one illustration of a life dedicated to the improving his community and society. His civic leadership offers us a model for uniting success in our professional lives with advancing justice and opportunity for all persons. His career as a businessman and civic leader inspire and exemplify a life well-lived. I am privileged to introduce this book with a few words about how all of us, especially young men and women embarking on their careers, can benefit from Cabell's eighty years of experience.

Remarkably, Cabell, despite his age, has not withdrawn from his lifetime of involvement in civic affairs. After retiring from his business in 1986, Cabell increased the time he devoted to civic affairs from twenty per-cent of the workweek to nearly full time. Readers will notice that Cabell and his wife Shirley have become even more of a collaborative team in their civic involvement during the last two decades. They simultaneously devote much attention to their family, another important contribution to our collective future. Cabell has continued participation in the National Academy of Sciences and a multitude of other organizations. His recent projects include serving on an advisory committee for the Shepherd Program on Poverty and Human Capability at Washington and Lee and leadership for the Jonathan Daniels Award committee at Virginia Military Institute, Cabell's alma mater. His investment of time and energy in preparing this entirely revised second edition of this volume is yet another instance of Cabell's nearly seven decades of leadership. Cabell goes beyond contributing his own leadership; he galvanizes all of us to improve the communities and the society in which we reside.

When Howard Packett, a businessman and civic leader from Roanoke, Virginia, introduced Tom Shepherd and me to Cabell in 1999, we did not imagine that he would become a decade-long advisor and advocate for the Shepherd Program. He was, after all, a successful retired businessman and civic leader in his seventh decade. We hoped at best for a little sage advice based on Cabell's experience as chair of the board of Total Action Against Poverty, the community action agency for the Roanoke Valley, and modest financial support. When the vision of a higher education program to study and act to diminish poverty and expand human capability captured Cabell's attention, he became a tenacious advocate for the program to anyone who would listen— and as will become apparent to readers of this book, many persons listen to Cabell. He has been a valued adviser for new directions to enhance the education of students and their first-hand participation in direct efforts to diminish poverty. Cabell has drawn on the experience of decades of civic involvement that has fostered yet another project that begins locally but has global implications. Astonishingly, he has simultaneously been involved in fostering the Jonathan Daniels prize at VMI to recognize national leadership for racial and social justice— former President Carter and Andrew Young have been recipients—and in advancing the work of the Cabell Brand Center for International Poverty and Resource Studies at Roanoke College in Salem, Virginia. These are only his projects in higher education. Other efforts by Cabell have focused more directly on economic justice and sustainable development, the words abbreviated on Cabell and Shirley's Virginia license plate.

Even in his ninth decade, Cabell undertakes new projects, as revealed in the revised seventh and culminating chapter on peace and human rights in this volume. That chapter offers a fitting conclusion to Cabell's charge to us for two reasons. First, reminiscence of Martin Luther King, Jr., Cabell believes that addressing the challenges of poverty, education, health, the environment, and racial justice are integral to peace. Peace is possible, Cabell contends, only if we give simultaneous attention to the other social problems he considers in this book. Second, in addition to his ongoing active support for the Shepherd Program, Cabell now devotes most of his considerable energy to civic and political leadership to promote peace, such as a recent visit with Shirley to President Oscar Arias in Costa Rica and his involvement with the Institute for Peace Educational Center in Washington, D.C. For Cabell working to diminish poverty and to secure peace go hand-in-hand.

His tireless advocacy of the Shepherd Program reinforces his effort for peace. Cabell has also been instrumental in promoting the multi-school Shepherd Consortium for the study of poverty in higher education that we anticipate emerging in the next year. Like the Shepherd Program at Washington and Lee, the Consortium will seek to prepare future professional and civic leaders to contribute significantly to advancing capability and reducing poverty. Cabell's story in this volume exemplifies our hope for graduates of these programs of study and learning through first-hand involvement. His business life with Stuart McGuire challenged barriers to racial equity and promoted adequate healthcare and flexible work schedules to enable a flourishing family and personal life for employees. His civic involvement—never less than one-fifth of his work week (a significant tithe of his productive energy)—addresses the social and other barriers that limit the effective freedom of the most disadvantaged members of society to achieve reasonable goals. Cabell has been constantly mindful that dedication to these ends advances the common good of society as well as serves the needs of persons impeded by poverty. Enlightened and prudent engagement suffuses his professional and civic life.

Cabell is not a do-gooder who eschews controversy. His story is one of courage to take unpopular social, political, and even moral stands as part of his energetic leadership. He has taken risks as a socially conscious and prudent businessman and as a civic leader. He is opinionated, but his opinions are informed by knowledge of the issues he addresses. The point of this volume should not be for every reader to embrace Cabell's politics or even his policy judgments—although such agreement would undoubtedly please him—but for readers to realize that professional and civic contributions require more than doing nice things by apolitical and non-controversial actions. To make a difference, professional and civic leaders must be informed about social, policy, and political issues. Effective leaders wish flourishing for every member of society and seek to advance the common good, but wishing for good things is not enough. They must also follow Cabell in forming visions for what could be, making judgments, and having the courage to act on their evolving judgments. Cabell's life provides a model for informed and courageous actions. Those who do not join in espousing his exact political and policy judgments must nevertheless be knowledgeable and courageous to be effective. Emulation does not necessarily imitate, but embodying Cabell's example requires a willingness to sacrifice popular acceptance in order to pursue an informed, albeit imperfect, conception of the right.

This narrative covering over seventy years also reminds us that an engaged life does not begin with dinner with the President. Cabell's professional and civic life began modestly and locally. His early involvement led to an ever-enlarging network of friends and associates who became partners in advancing social causes that they shared with Cabell. Nor did Cabell first gain influence and power and then later decide to devote his influence to good ends. He gained friends and influence by contributing to the social good, and these contributions put him in a position to make a difference in the national and international arenas and to better serve his local community. Cabell clearly gains pleasure and satisfaction from his wide range of friends and associations. His leadership in service redounded to his well-being, but it began with a desire to foster the community and the lives of others rather than seeking personal influence and happiness.

This book focuses especially on young people blessed with the capability to achieve many of their goals. Although religion is not a prominent explicit theme in this story, Cabell constantly reminds us that he has always been the undeserving beneficiary of good fortune, both in his achievements and in his recognitions and material successes. His formation in the Presbyterian Church has undoubtedly shaped a view that recipients of grace are obligated to dedicate their gifts to the benefit of others, especially those not so fortunate, and to society. Although Cabell avoids self-righteous exhortation to duty, this account of his life conveys a sense of obligation, not merely an invitation to volunteer, to engage in professional and civic efforts to advance justice and the common good. Cabell's story is not about nobility condescending to help others. It is about doing what justice requires.

My hope for this volume is that readers will take away more than a call to action, although it is an inspiration to do more for our communities. Cabell's story is also a model for how our professional and civic lives can, in collaboration with our fellow citizens, foster at least a minimal capability for our fellow humans, improve our environment, advance racial justice and harmony, and displace violence with a just peace. As this revised edition continues to inspire and teaches its readers, this latest effort by Cabell, probably not his last, adds one more achievement to a lifetime of improving his community, society, and the world.

Cabell's seemingly indefatigable labors for justice and the common good were energized by the publication of the first edition of this volume. He has spoken with multiple groups of students who read the book, including hundreds of students at Baylor University in Texas. The book and visit to Texas, helped inspire the partners of Bridgeway Capital Management, a firm in Houston founded on philanthropic and civic commitments, to adopt a company policy that each partner will devote one-fifth of his or her workweek to civic involvement and leadership. Cabell will undoubtedly follow the publication of this second edition by accepting invitations to talk personally with student readers of the volume about their aspirations as future professional and civic leaders.

Dr. Harlan Beckley
Director, Shepherd Program on Poverty and Human Capability
Fletcher Otey Thomas Professor of Religion
Washington and Lee University

Foreword

by E. Cabell Brand

Societies are cooperative ventures, each generation receiving, developing, nurturing and passing on the triumphs, tragedies, hopes and challenges that constitute the flow of history. Those of us who have lived long and fruitful lives have a duty to convey experiences and lessons we've learned to those who will assume from us society's positions of leadership.

As a business executive and still an active participant in the business, civic and environmental life of my local, state, national and international communities, I wish to share some insights I've gained with young people just beginning their careers. Although I believe these experiences and insights regarding certain deep, core values will be broadly appealing, the specific target audience certainly would comprise aspiring young business executives with whom I expect I will have much in common. I hope that my experiences will exhort those young men and women to develop a deep appreciation for the benefits of getting involved in the larger community even as they establish the crucial foundations of their own successful careers. For this reason, I have chosen to entitle this book using the enduring words of Robert F. Kennedy: "If not me, who? If not now, when?"

This book originally was written before Barak Obama's election as president; before the onset of the serious financial crisis our country is still facing; before all of the stimulus money had been appropriated; before the banking crisis and the failure of a number of banking institutions like Lehman Brothers and Bear Stearns; before unemployment reached 10 percent; before the continuing health care crisis was debated for more than a year in protracted congressional stalemate; before the Afghanistan troop build-up.

However, none of these changes affects the thesis of this book. It has become even more important that everyone in our society get involved at least locally and at every level of activity that they can to strengthen our society and build a bottoms-up leadership system.

That is the theme of this book: Get involved.

These crises before our nation in fact give each of us an additional opportunity and an additional urgency to get involved. We all need to insist that our elected political leaders do what's right for the country and not what's right for their own re-election.

If we don't do it, how will it be done?

I have revised and updated many parts of this book, but the theme is the same. I have added to the appendix a few articles and letters that I have written during these crises, some of those mentioned above. I add new examples of other ways that we can get involved with local action. We need to let our leaders know how we feel and insist that every elected official use his or her best judgment to do the right thing for our country.

The first article in the appendix was written in March of 2009, about 60 days after President Obama took office. As a businessman and a former bank director, I have strong opinions as to what needed to be done then. I have strong opinions today about what still needs to be done, proposed actions that I will address throughout the book as we discuss each of the six challenges I see before us.

It's interesting that I would not change very much that I wrote in March of 2009 from my recommendations today. I made the categorical statement that the government should let the giant insurance corporation AIG go bankrupt the same way that Lehman Brothers and Bear Stearns went bankrupt, or to sell out. There have been many articles and analyses of the AIG bailout, some of which have even called it a "Goldman Sachs bailout." Some commentators have even said that former Treasury Secretary Henry Paulson had a conflict of interest as former chief financial officer of Goldman Sachs in the way the bailout money was used. The AIG issue is very complicated, because that company had many different divisions, and it was really only one major division that caused it to lose so much money.

The reasons I've gone into such detail here on this particular crisis is because it gets to the heart of every problem we'll discuss in the following pages, and that is the role of government in our society. What is the role of a government in regulating financial institutions, guaranteeing jobs, providing unemployment compensation, improving our education system, implementing national health insurance, protecting our environment, insisting on racial justice and enacting global policies to safeguard peace and protect human rights? I will discuss this theme in each of the subsequent chapters.

In more than eight decades of living and enjoying what our culture would recognize as a successful life, I have come to realize that the single greatest attribute of a great and just society is the assurance of opportunity for all. I know that not all people are born with the same inherent talents and abilities. Not all people are born into the same circumstances. Some of us enter the world blessed with good fortune and privilege; others of us arrive under less-fortunate, perhaps even grim, circumstances of disability and poverty. Fate may deal a generous hand or, as we must recognize even in this richly endowed country, it may impose cruel burdens of material, mental or emotional deficiency.

But I have come to believe that we are all in this enterprise together, making the best we can of our common lot with all humankind sharing this planet. I have come to believe that we have within our power — our intellect, our experience, our technology, our connectedness as human beings — to make the world a better, more promising place for us and for those who will come after us. Indeed, I believe we have a moral as well as a practical obligation to do so. I have learned not to trust the easy instinct toward premature judgment. Many people lack a basic understanding of the plight of others who, for reasons often beyond their control, find themselves in the misfortune of poverty. Some people, unfortunately, are so captive of their ignorance that they simply don't care. Failing, much less refusing, to understand and care about the plight of so many is especially self-defeating in a society that proclaims its dedication to equal opportunity for everyone.

From nearly half a century of founding and working with community action agencies, I have learned that almost every man and woman desires to succeed. They just need a chance. I have experienced the satisfaction of helping to fulfill the hopes and aspirations of people seeking a "hand up," and not a handout. When those who are weak are made stronger, then the community's shared burdens — and its opportunities — become not only more bearable but also more promising and productive.

Franklin D. Roosevelt seemed to understand this basic civic truth almost instinctively. He knew that a robust society would remain that way only if the door were open for everyone to contribute to the "common welfare" as well as to enjoy the fruits of general prosperity. The New Deal eventually widened that door to a growing middle class that became the measure worldwide of social and economic progress. John F. Kennedy advanced that vision by opening broader vistas through a New Frontier of opportunity. Lyndon Johnson sought to extend further the promise of the "hand up" in the "War Against Poverty."

Public initiatives that gradually began to improve educational and economic opportunity, from the New Deal through the Great Society, were critical in shaping my understanding of the workings of a just, productive and prosperous society. I was formed as a young man during the Depression. I fought in World War II and in its aftermath worked in the U.S. diplomatic corps in Germany to help implement the Marshall Plan, the great, historic example of the "hand up" that helped to restore war-ravaged countries around the world. That U.S.-led international act of "generosity" illustrated the wisdom and prudence of investing in the "common interest." America became stronger and freer because it had helped other nations to become stronger and freer. Later, as a struggling young businessman, I realized that waiting for someone else to create opportunities was a selfish delusion. Expanding the threshold in which more people could participate in the civic and economic life of the community was, I discovered, not only likely to produce a stronger citizenry but, as a strictly practical matter, was also in my own enlightened self-interest.

At various points in the history of America, generations have built upon and advanced those ringing ideals expressed in our Declaration of Independence and the Constitution, especially the Bill of Rights. Yes, those ideals were more easily expressed than realized, often painfully achieved over time against the grudging resistance of prejudice, self-interest and blind custom. But America's story has been an unfolding narrative in which succeeding generations struggled to reaffirm the hopes and dreams our founders proclaimed, even though they left it to "our posterity" to forge into reality what their noble words proclaimed.

I have come to the present stage of my life, however, concerned that America has lost its way. Increasingly, our national policies reflect an abandonment of the principles of the "general welfare" and "common purpose." Rather than offering a "hand up," I see a weakening of the civic bonds that hold us all together in our commitment to education, economic opportunity and preservation of our common home: Planet Earth. As critically important as individual initiative and self-reliance are to developing well-grounded, productive individuals, history has taught our nation that its noblest achievements have come from the unity of purpose that can be forged only in a society strong enough to nurture and sustain a culture of equal opportunity for all.

This republic and its capitalist, free-enterprise economy have allowed me to enjoy good fortune in so many ways. Yet I have always been aware that I stand on the shoulders of those who came before me, who set inspiring examples and who secured the legal, civic and institutional safeguards so essential to the workings of a just and prosperous society. As a result, I've always believed that the current generation should be doing all it can to develop strong shoulders to give a similar boost to those who follow us.

Yet poverty remains a stubborn challenge in our world, and the United States is by no means exempt from its socially and economically corrosive effects. Recent statistics from the U.S. Census Bureau indicate that nearly 18 percent of Americans younger than 18 live in poverty. Left uncorrected, that is a troubling prospect for the near future. In addition, globalization of the economy poses long-term potential to harm the fabric of society if we fail to assist the transitions of those whose livelihoods are threatened by weakened or disappearing industries. I don't believe we can afford to stand by while such a significant proportion of fellow Americans slip further from their ability to pursue their hopes and aspirations. Poverty is costly. Prisons, social services of all sorts, unnecessary health problems, social alienation and the consequences of family violence are expensive for everyone in society. From my experience, it is cheaper to pay the costs of attacking and diminishing poverty on the front end than by paying for it at the back end. I prefer to think of it as investing in the long-term, widespread revitalization of the just, vibrant society we all want.

Those who have prospered from the opportunities afforded to us should never become "too busy" to recognize how important a strong society is to the economic vitality of the nation. In my more than 40 years of involvement with efforts to alleviate the consequences of poverty and environmental degradation, I was often asked why I devoted 20 percent of my time to such initiatives when my only apparent gain has been the satisfaction of helping people who needed some help. I could quote Scripture passages about feeding the hungry, giving drink to the thirsty, healing the sick, visiting those in prison and other acts of "charity." Such an argument in itself would be compelling for many, but I also am realist enough to advocate pragmatism as a worthy companion of idealism. I have been a businessman, a capitalist. I believe in free enterprise. I believe that those of us who do participate fully in our society must figure out a way to help those who do not, so they won't become so alienated that they begin to harbor destructive anti-social resentments. An equal-opportunity society, living under democratic principles and the rule of law, takes prudent measures to provide everyone the opportunity to have a stake in the community's shared future.

I have noted hopeful signs in the last few years of a spirit of self-interested civic generosity among certain young men and women, especially in my participation with the leadership programs at Virginia Military Institute and Washington and Lee University. Such virtues should be encouraged. These are our country's future leaders, and I've taken great satisfaction talking with them and learning about their ideals, hopes and expectations. I make it a point to ask these young potential leaders: What kind of goals in life do you intend to set for yourself, besides simply making money? What kind of world do you want to build for your children? So many of them exhibit a praiseworthy maturity, expressing not only their aspirations for personal career success but also a desire to make a favorable difference in leaving the world a better place for those generations to come. I believe such responses are a source of great hope. These young people have lived their entire lives in a culture reverberating with the barrage of messages worshiping "me." A new generation, I believe, is responding to their world now by confronting problems that require "we" as an essential part of the solutions.

The chapters that follow are intended to offer examples of how in my business and civic career I sought to identify certain barriers to a better life and organize local efforts to help communities overcome "universal" problems. That is, I have sought to provide opportunities that allow people to think globally and to act locally. In my mind, that is the most effective way to reduce great problems to manageable size and bring the understanding and creativity of dedicated people to bear on the lives of their neighbors.

As anyone with only a modest reading of history knows, problems are a constant in the human experience, and efforts ebb and flow in various generations' dedication to attacking their common challenges. As I have indicated, I think the current generation of political and economic leadership in our country has lost its way, abandoning many of the values that I believe are essential to broad participation in the "general welfare" of our nation and the other civic ideals enumerated in the Preamble of the Constitution. So I am urging a new generation to take up the torch and to lead our return to the path toward greater opportunity for everyone, including the growing numbers of the dispossessed who are beginning to lose ground. I believe it is crucial to keep faith with those who paved the way for us, who gave meaning and purpose to the phrase "equal opportunity," and I hope in this book to challenge, exhort and encourage all — regardless of the generation into which they were born — who desire to keep that faith as they fashion the strategies to confront age-old problems with imagination, innovation, determination and vigor.

My personal response was to become earnestly involved with what was then a new concept, the federally sponsored community action movement. I remain committed to those programs I helped to inaugurate and that have evolved and are still serving my community more than 40 years later. The specific problems may differ in various degrees from those we took on in 1965, but the nature of addressing basic human needs always remains. Some of those problems, partly because of their inherent nature but also because of social and political indifference and neglect in the last several years, now present what may prove to be a crisis if they are not addressed seriously and soon. From my own involvement and experience, I will offer examples in the chapters that follow of how we took on certain problems. Those experiences, I hope, may provide some useful illustrations and insights about how we went about trying to reverse particular social, economic and environmental deficiencies. But even more important to me, I also intend to direct attention to the current consequences of failing to keep faith with our most enduring democratic values and ideals. Redressing those breaches of faith — in the service of our children, our hope and our future — now falls to a new generation. Peace, justice and prosperity don't just happen. They are the result of vision, commitment to each other and old-fashioned hard work. What worked in terms of program and organizational structure in the 1960s, '70s and '80s may differ somewhat in the twenty-first century, but such challenges are hardly insurmountable for minds determined to find solutions and hearts open wide enough to match pragmatism with idealism.

No achievement of enduring value in life — personal, corporate, civic — is possible without effort, struggle and difficulty. I have known the uncertainty of a growing business under financial strain. I have been the target of debasement and threats arising from bigotry and racial enmity. I have suffered the agony of the tragic deaths of four children. Yet those ordeals opened to me priceless insights and taught me valuable lessons about patience, perseverance, resilience and determination.

I hope that those who read this book will come to appreciate, as I have, that each generation contributes to our "more perfect union" when dedicated people respond to their world by confronting problems that require "we," not just "me," as an essential part of building an enduring, prosperous and just future for ourselves and those who will follow.

Chapter One

Getting Involved Personally: If Not Me, Then Who?

One evening at the elegant Washington Sheraton Hotel in 1998, my wife Shirley and I attended a private dinner hosted by President Bill Clinton. As it happened, we were seated at the same table with President Clinton. At one point, I asked him, "Mr. President, I have a question for you." He looked across the table at me and replied, "Yes, Mr. Brand."

At that moment, an aide came up to the president and informed him that the time had come for him to address the group. I thought I'd missed my chance to ask my question. An hour later, when Clinton had finished speaking, he looked across the room, saw me in the audience and returned to our table. "Mr. Brand," he said, "you never had a chance to ask me that question."

I said, "Well, thank you, Mr. President. My question is, why did you in your budget cut the Community Service Block Grants, which fund a thousand community action agencies in the United States?" And he said, "I don't know anything about that. You go see Frederick Raines over at the next table. He's head of the Office of Management and Budget, and ask him." And I said, "Mr. President, would you go with me?" And he said, "Yes." So we went over to Raines and asked him, and he said he didn't know anything about it. So I told him that it was a tragedy to cut this budget because this money was leveraged more than 20 times locally and dealt with poor people and needed to

1

be restored and eventually increased. With the president of the United States standing there, Raines said, "Well, I will look into it."

Since it was not a huge amount of money in the federal budget, relatively speaking, it was fully restored and has remained about at that level ever since with constant lobbying of the Congress, even during Republican administrations.

That successful encounter occurred not simply because I was in the room with the president at the right time and under the right circumstances. That meeting happened only because I had been involved in a long train of events that began decades before: getting involved in local civic organizations and local politics. I was instrumental in the organization in 1965 of one of those thousands of community action agencies back home in the Roanoke Valley of Southwestern Virginia. I had participated in politics, including making modest financial contributions to candidates and officeholders, from the local to the national level. The point is, had I not been so involved, I never would have had the opportunity to be at that dinner in our nation's capital and advocate a change that was critical for local community action agencies across the country — including the one I had helped to organize in Roanoke, Total Action Against Poverty, or TAP.

In a vital, wholesome society, good things don't just happen by accident. They happen because concerned, dedicated and inventive people decide to make their own lives and those of their fellow citizens better by coming together to make good things happen. Getting involved in local activities, whether it be with nonprofit organizations, political, civic or other associations, starts with a personal commitment to participate in our society.

Making those decisions to become engaged should begin as early in a career as possible, so that each experience helps to nurture and reinforce those that will make even greater contributions at each new commitment of service. I have discovered in my own life two critical, mutually reinforcing reasons why such decisions are essential. First, I have found that being active in local organizations has led to opportunities to become involved both nationally and globally, which has added great meaning and satisfaction to my life. Second, so much needs to be done in our society. Today, I think we have lost sight of the core values of the country, what once seemed to me the very promise of

America. There are so many things that need to be addressed: broader economic opportunity, improved education, health care, environmental safeguards, racial and social injustice, the environment and, of course, peace. But the point is that the solution to each of these problems can, should, and must start locally, forming the impetus for nationwide mass movements to achieve those aspects of American life that still await fulfillment. The people of our democracy should demand that our leaders act in ways consistent with the spirit as well as the letter of our Constitution. Making that message heard will require getting involved locally.

This notion first came to me in 1947, when I had finally graduated from Virginia Military Institute after my education there had been interrupted by service with the Army in World War II. Having experienced the ravages of combat, the utter destruction of so much of Europe, and the plight of concentration camp prisoners, I decided to return with the Foreign Service in the State Department to Germany to assist with implementing the Marshall Plan of European reconstruction. And, to be candid, having fallen in love during the war also had something to do with my decision, as I intended to go back and get married, which I did.

For the next two years, I received the unanticipated opportunity of living in Berlin during the Berlin blockade and seeing first-hand the difference between a democratic West Berlin and a socialistic, communistic, totalitarian-led East Berlin. That experience had a dramatic effect on my life. Because I had seen so much destruction, destitution and misery in Germany, France and other parts of Western Europe, I was deeply impressed by what was being done in the postwar reconstruction.

In 1949, I decided to resign from the Foreign Service, although my work under the Marshall Plan showed me the importance of the United States as a bulwark of hope in the world. At that point, I decided to return home and contribute to strengthening the society that I believed could become an even greater force for good. I first had to get a job, but I concluded that I would spend some significant part of my time doing something of value in my local community. Since the average work week was five days, I decided that I would allocate one full day toward helping in the community doing important things. This was 20 percent of my time. I'm proud, frankly, to say that I continued with that time allocation for the next 40 years.

I had no idea in 1949 what my career would be. When I graduated from VMI, I had been offered a wonderful opportunity with the General Electric Co., and I assumed that I could come back and apply to that company for a position. But I never lost sight of that decision to devote 20 percent of my time to doing things, particularly locally, to correct or prevent some of the sources of human neglect and deprivation that I had seen so starkly during and after the war.

So I came home with my wife and dog and moved in with my parents. My father asked me what I intended to do. I said I didn't know, but that I was going to apply at General Electric, which had a local branch. I then found out that he was liquidating his door-to-door shoe sales business, even though he had recently developed a new type of shoe, which I thought could be sold and the enterprise probably even expanded. He said, though, that he was tired and didn't want to undertake restructuring of the business himself. For the next week I studied the prospects for success and made a formal business arrangement with him. Then I got the approval of my brothers and sisters to try to avoid future family conflicts.

For the next 40 years, until we sold the business in 1986, I worked very hard in the business world. But I never forgot my 1949 commitment and took advantage of every opportunity I had to join local organizations. Early on, I developed my little black book with my calendar. In that book — which I still keep handy — I allocated time around my business, family and other activities in contributing locally to community needs, a practice that ultimately opened national and global opportunities to me.

In the early 1950s, I was asked to help organize a Salem Rotary Club. My grandfather and father had been members of the Rotary Club in Roanoke, but a few business leaders in neighboring Salem had expressed interest in forming their own organization. In the process of building our new shoe business, I saw the value of contributing to the civic foundation of the city where I was building both a business and a home and agreed to participate. In time, I would become president of the Salem Rotary Club.

Among our first projects to serve the needs of Salem was the restoration of the East Hill Cemetery, which was situated at the city's east entrance and where my Grandmother and Grandfather Brand are buried. As a boy, I would go with my father and grandfather to visit the family plot, which they had paid someone to keep mowed and groomed. Over more than a century since its establishment and with no clear indication of ownership other than for individual burial plots, much of the rest of the cemetery lacked such care. No one was taking care of the remainder of the property. By the 1950s, weeds proliferated, some nearly as tall as I was. I proposed that our new Salem Rotary Club join the Salem Chamber of Commerce in a partnership to clean up the cemetery. Unfortunately, the chamber decided to let the Rotarians take on the project alone, which we did. Club members performed about 90 percent of the hard work, on weekends and evenings over nearly six months. When the work was completed, I helped to arrange an agreement with the Salem City Council to convey to the local government ownership and responsibility for its care, which continues to this day.

A few years after helping start the Rotary Club, I was asked to help form a Torch Club, a small discussion group of professional people who write papers and conduct discussions six or seven times a year on topical issues of importance to them. I agreed to help organize the local chapter, eventually became its president and am still a member.

As a result of these activities, which occurred during the course of expanding our business, I was invited to be a member of the Council of Community Services of the Roanoke Valley, which oversaw all of the United Way activities and studied each of the non-profit groups in the valley. In this role, I had the opportunity to analyze the Economic Opportunity Act of 1964. In a council meeting one day, a member of the committee stood up and wanted to make a motion that under no circumstances would the Roanoke Valley and our council ever want to participate in what he called this "boondoggle" called the "Poverty Program" that had just been passed in Washington. Instinctively I knew that if this gentleman was against something, I was probably for it. So I asked to table that motion and get a copy of the legislation and study it before we voted on it. Everyone agreed. So I called our local congressman, who was a Republican, and asked for 30 copies of the Economic Opportunity Act of 1964. He wanted to know what I wanted them for. I said I wanted to study them. To make a long story short, we studied it and decided in 1965 to start a community action agency, Total Action Against Poverty, or TAP, which provided some 40 programs, including Head Start, the first integrated school in the Roanoke Valley. Throughout its history, TAP has spun off more than 10 separate, self-sustaining nonprofit organizations, such as the food bank and the child health investment program.

But the point of all this is that if I had not been involved in the activities enumerated thus far, I never would have been invited to serve on that particular committee and never would have had the opportunity to start TAP.

As the late U.S. House Speaker Tip O'Neill once said, "All politics is local." Continuing to seek ever more ways to become involved locally, I joined the Salem Democratic Party, participated in supporting state candidates and political initiatives and eventually took an interest in national politics as well. As a result of my active role in state politics, Gov. Chuck Robb asked me in 1984 to serve on the state Board of Health, and I eventually became its chairman, from 1989 to 1993. In that position, I was fortunate to become very much aware at the state level of the implications of many shortcomings in the American health-care system. That understanding helped me to form many of the ideas and policies that have become the foundation of what began as a local and later a statewide program in Virginia, and which now forms the basis for the federal Children's Health Insurance Program, or CHIP.

It's not unique that being involved in a local Rotary Club or local chamber of commerce, a local community action agency and other local civic and political organizations led to being involved in the state and national organizations of that type. As a result of my local participation, I got involved in Rotary International at the district level, in the National Chamber of Commerce and in the community action and economic opportunity programs at the national level. In the course of those activities, I was able to meet Sargent Shriver and other important people who led the community action movement nationwide. One thing led to another — and another and another.

I served on several committees of the U.S. Chamber of Commerce and was an active member of its Council on Trends and Perspectives, which looked at society in general and the problems of those who don't participate in our society. I was an associate at the Conference Board, the President's Circle of the National Academy of Sciences, the Heinz Center for Science, Economics and the Environment and the World Resources Institute. In part as a result of some of those experiences, I was fortunate to participate in several initiatives involved with President Jimmy Carter and activities at the Carter Center.

For many of those years, I was a member of the Young Presidents Organization, but at that time eligibility ended at age 50, so I joined the World Presidents Organization and the Chief Executives Organization, eventually expanding my personal scope of activity to include the international sphere. Thinking globally and acting locally, I realized then, became a self-reinforcing cycle of opportunity.

I am heartened by one dimension of getting involved locally that I am beginning to see more and more: the assumption of social responsibility by businesses and other organizations, especially banks and other public corporations that are encouraging their employees to engage in community service. Such commitment not only improves the image of those businesses in their communities but also contributes to the betterment of the social as well as economic conditions where they live and work. This is important because there is so much to do. The fiscal system of the United States is in trouble. We have a huge debt, and ongoing military expenses, and we have no plan to pay off our debts. The health-care system is still in trouble with many Americans without any health insurance, and an even greater number faced with inadequate access to health care. State and local resources are limited, and the infrastructure of this country is crumbling. The environment is a huge problem, as are the racial and social justice issues. Our education system needs a complete overhaul. In some cities, 50 percent of the high school students do not graduate. In Southwest Virginia where I live, 30 percent of all working-age adults do not have a high school education.

All of these problems need the attention and resolve of each of us, beginning right now. We can get involved in some fashion with organizations and movements that are dealing with such issues. This is what our democracy is all about and is the way that we can work hard every day, dedicating a percentage of our time to make our country better and our society stronger for our grandchildren. That's why I'm as active as I'm able to be at my age, trying to create a better life for our 13 grandchildren.

If each person, regardless of career, would get involved actively in one or more local organizations, mass movements could gradually coalesce to overcome society's major deficiencies and shortcomings. It's easy to say, "I don't have time." Nobody has enough time. But I learned time management first at VMI, by creating my little black book with my schedule and time-allocations for each day, each month, and making a five-year plan. That way, you find time to do the things you think are important.

Someone told me lately we've lost sight of our core values and how to connect them in the way we live. I was struck by the relevance of a statement by Anthony Romero, executive director of the American Civil Liberties Union: "Will this be the time for the much-needed renewal of America's commitment to justice, fairness and the rule of law? This much we know for certain: The answer is up to us. We cannot rely on the wisdom or courage of political leaders to guide us. We cannot count on the simple passage of time to heal the damage. We have to take matters in our own hands and make the defense of freedom our own highly personal mission."

We all should reject passing the buck to others as an unacceptable option. I know that my own early engagements with civic challenges opened my eyes to the understanding that being involved locally gets you eventually involved nationally and perhaps globally. What you learn from this series of participations helps you strengthen the local organization by applying what you've learned about what goes on elsewhere, and with a more national or global perspective.

You can do the same thing today, if you will make a commitment to spend a percentage of your time in one, two or even three local organizations to become an integral part of improving their missions, whether it's your church, civic club, political organization or other community-based group. Nothing opens the eye to solutions for common challenges better than making an uncommon commitment to getting involved personally to make a positive difference.

Had I not been involved locally in poverty programs and in local politics, and had I not participated in so many other related activities over the years, I never would have had the opportunity to be at the dinner with the president of the United States and do something at the national level that would help low-income people.

At the state level, because I was involved in the political process, I was able to lobby to get different programs included as line items in the state budget. Such initiatives include the Child Health Insurance Program, Project Discovery, Virginia CARES, the Virginia Water Project and others, all still important facets of Virginia's commitment to reducing poverty and its consequences. The point of this seems clear to me: American society needs the active interest, participation, ideas and energy of everyone, not just those who have vital business interests or only those who have substantial financial resources, but everyone. It's not too late when you retire to do things for the League of Older Americans, the Food Bank and other worthwhile organizations.

America is a generous nation. But the strength of our democracy and our free-enterprise system lies within the individual people in the local community, where everything starts. Devote your active involvement to those causes that most interest you, but also spend a considerable amount of time helping local organizations and even start new, worthwhile activities. Those contributions add a dimension to your life that you not only will never regret but that also fill your life with a greater sense of purpose, meaning and happiness. I believe that as a result of such activities, our communities are stronger and our nation itself is stronger and more resilient.

Chapter Two

Economic Opportunity and Justice:
Making Our Efforts Count

E arly experiences in almost everyone's life influence the way people look at the world, assess their place in it and form their expectations of what that world has to offer. So much of the way I have tried in my business and civic careers to confront the shortcomings of inequality has been motivated by what I experienced growing up in the segregated South. An entire segment of our population lacked essential access to the opportunities I expected as a matter of course.

I felt many times, even within my own family, a deep, abiding frustration with attitudes and conditions that struck me as fundamentally unfair. Even as I felt fortunate to be blessed with talent, ambition and a strong work ethic that served me well beginning in my student days at Virginia Military Institute, I could not escape my unease with the self-defeating logic of discrimination.

These perceptions of the consequences of racial injustice broadened when I witnessed first-hand the Nazi threat to the world. As a young Army officer, I saw the destruction of cities in Western Europe, the horrible civilian casualties, the tragedy of war itself. I came into direct contact with Germans who had been headed for the concentration camps and gas chambers. When the war ended, I also saw the wisdom — hard-learned from the diplomatic and economic failures after World War I — of rejuvenating a war-torn continent through the Marshall

Plan. For two years after the war, I had the opportunity with the State Department in Berlin to see the difference between democratic and totalitarian governments and the resolve of the United States to stand up to the Soviet Union during the Berlin blockade.

By 1949, I had decided to leave government service and go into business. My goal was to provide economic security for my family but also to spend at least 20 percent of my time to strengthen the U.S. free-enterprise society. After seeing the horrible consequences of tyranny under the Nazis, and seeing the commendable but painfully gradual progress made by the Marshall Plan's restoration, I recognized the importance of building and improving a nation through the vast efforts of a committed civil society. So I decided to return to the United States, go into the private sector and learn what I could do to get involved and build a better life for me, my family and my neighbors. This basic challenge confronts all young Americans as they take those first steps toward a career and the life they will build for the future, regardless of what field they may choose to enter. I also firmly believe that they will discover value in abundance not only in their careers but also in the vibrancy of life in their communities and in their own personal gratification for having contributed to a spirit of common purpose. All that is necessary is to recognize opportunities and to seize them.

In the next 30 years, I was fortunate to be presented with two unusual opportunities. One was to take over a small shoe business, build it up and take it public. Then, a year after passage of the Economic Opportunity Act of 1964, I helped start a community action agency and the Head Start program.

Once I had made the basic commitment to spend 20 percent of my time — the equivalent of a single workday per week — serving society on local issues, I learned that it's easy to experiment with different projects, and to do so with great satisfaction. In my case, it was helping to start a Rotary Club and serving on local and national chambers of commerce, the local United Way and other civic organizations.

All the civic activities, especially those directed toward reducing poverty, drew upon the skills and disciplines that I had developed in building and expanding the business. To the thoughtful person with a little creativity, all such skills are transferable. In turn, I realized that a commitment to increasing economic opportunity and increasing participation by those who have been dealt a poor hand in life offer mutually reinforcing benefits possible only when everyone feels a sense of ownership, with a stake in the community. Applying practical career lessons and opening doors for civic opportunity to everyone strikes me as one of those primary articles of faith necessary to guide those who want to build and sustain a just and prosperous society.

My personal career lessons, you might say, started literally from the ground up. In 1949, the Ortho-Vent Shoe Company — founded in 1904 by my grandfather as the Brand Shoe Company — had five employees and about 50 part-time sales people nationally. Over the next 20 years, we were able to build this door-to-door shoe-selling business to more than 100,000 part-time salesmen and 1,000 local employees. In 1970, we took the company public after deploying a five-year plan to compound earnings growth 20 percent a year and have a minimum profit requirement for the public offering. All of that was with the same business model of selling shoes door-to-door. Almost as soon as the company went public, direct-sales marketing conditions changed drastically, and we were forced to modify our business model and develop mail-order companies to supplement the door-to-door business. Later, we added a marketing distribution center to ship products for other companies.

Those challenging decisions under relentless market stress led us to ask constantly, "What business are we in?" That process laid the foundation for evaluating *any* undertaking — a profit-seeking business or a social-services agency — that relied for its effectiveness on the most efficient adjustment of corporate resources.

Some insights into how we developed our business in a dynamic, rapidly evolving economy will help to illustrate the direct application of principles that apply to almost any human enterprise, whether producing and marketing a new line of shoes or creating opportunities to help people climb out of poverty and into a level of self-reliance and contribution to society.

My father worked as a salesman in the mid-1920s when he and my grandfather sensed that the wholesale business would soon be obsolete. They anticipated that manufacturers were going to sell their shoes directly to retailers, so they decided jointly to liquidate the business in 1926. My father took some of the assets from that business and decided to go into the door-to-door selling business, which two or three other companies already had begun. Although securing capital to support production and a central inventory was difficult during the Depression, the ability to recruit sales people was relatively easy because of the severe shortage of jobs. My father felt that creating a part-time sales force and drawing merchandise from a central inventory bypassed even the retail store and created the possibility of national distribution. This technique worked very well in the '20s and '30s. My father's business really boomed, because the Depression created an abundance of sales people who needed jobs. With World War II, shoes were in short supply because most of the factories were converted to making military shoes. Nevertheless, my father had established good relationships with suppliers since he decided to purchase his shoes from factories rather than invest in his own manufacturing facility. He purchased work shoes from one producer and men's dress shoes from another that specialized in a particular type of construction. When the war ended, the shoe shortage continued, driving pent-up demand, but then it became harder to recruit sales people. The economy was booming, America was rebuilding, and sales people could earn more money doing something other than take orders for shoes.

My father's business prospered from 1945 to 1948. Then, in 1949, the bottom fell out of the market. Supply began to catch up with demand, and salesmen were hard to recruit. About 40 part-time salesmen remained on my father's payroll, and they continued to sell shoes the best they could. But he saw the handwriting on the wall and the need to develop and print more elaborate catalogues, taking on more capital investment and risk. He was in the business almost by himself with just four employees at the time, so he decided that he would liquidate the business, sell his inventory, gather together what assets he had and retire. At about that time, I came home from World War II, looking for a job.

I had been offered a position with the local General Electric facility right after the war but had chosen to stay in Europe with the State Department administering the Marshall Plan recovery. By 1949, I realized that my future lay in the United States. My father had indicated that he intended to sell his business and retire. I asked to take a look at the books. In the process, I also examined my father's invention of the Spring Step cushion. This cushion could be easily and persuasively demonstrated to a potential customer and seemed to me an ideal product that would attract a sales force.

After going through the warehouse and looking at the shoes, I told my father I'd like to talk with the sales people around the country to better understand the market. He said he could not pay me very much, but he agreed to pay me $85 a month, which I supplemented by taking a correspondence course for the next three months under the GI Bill. I invested in a yellow four-door sedan and visited the sales people in North Carolina, the south of Alabama, Georgia, Mississippi, Louisiana, Tennessee, Kentucky, Illinois, Indiana, West Virginia and Virginia. I went to their homes and accompanied them in the field as they made their sales rounds. I even took a sample case myself and actually sold enough shoes to supplement my income and pay my expenses. This "tour," after my years in Europe, gave me an opportunity to see American society as it was in the post-war economy. Our salesmen were middle- and lower-class working people, most of whom received me graciously, asked me into their homes and invited me to have dinner with them.

By traveling with black as well as white salesmen, I discovered first-hand the problems of segregation, especially when taking one of the black men into a restaurant for a meal together. Such experiences gave me a first-hand view not only of the business but also of the need to make good on providing opportunities to help these people realize some of the fruits of the nation's bounty.

After about two months, I proposed to my father an arrangement to take over the business. Since I had two brothers and two sisters, I wanted to avoid future family disputes and proposed that my father and I sign a contract. He agreed to give me 40 percent of the business, and I would have the right to buy the rest of the stock at his total estimated value of the business at that time, which was $225,000. As time went on and the business grew, I was able to acquire 100 percent ownership by the time we went public.

During my travels to examine the sales territory, I learned that salesmen could realize a profit of only $2 or $3 per sale, so I decided to structure the nationwide sales force on a part-time basis as a means of providing additional income for ambitious workers. I streamlined a presentation, providing catalogues, sales books and Spring Step cushion samples that would help salesmen provide customers a brief, effective, convincing sales appeal — what I called the "two-minute demonstration." Because most of our sales were through the mail and paid by the customer through cash-on-delivery, or COD, I tried several different approaches and incentives to encourage prepayment on orders to reduce the company's exposure to cash-flow interruptions. That business model exposed the company to great uncertainty as to whether we might have to absorb losses from too many orders, for one reason or another, that customers might return. I sought to create incentives for customers to pre-pay their orders, a technique that eventually made up 40 percent of the business.

For more than a decade, I refined our business strategy, selecting the styles that would sell the best and developing dependable suppliers. Among my key business principles, I never wanted to take over more than 10 percent of the production of any one factory, so that neither the factory was dependent on us nor were we dependent on the factory. I also decided in the mid-1950s to change the name of the company from Ortho-Vent to Stuart McGuire, two names that had roots far back in our family tree, but also with what I considered a more marketable, sophisticated appeal as we broadened our business into mail-order clothing as well as shoes.

During the 1950s, we had enormous problems acquiring capital infusions into the business. We had to borrow money to produce the catalogues and support the inventory. We tried to diversify to two or three banks, but we had maximized our borrowing capacity with all the local banks. Eventually, we went to a national bank in Dallas, where my brother Hugh lived, and established a relationship that resulted in a larger line of credit. I knew, however, if the company were to prosper in the future, that we had to have a huge infusion of capital. The only way I knew to do that was to go public. So I began to study the process, traveling to New York to consult several leading investment banking firms.

As strenuous as guiding a growing business had been in those first dozen or so years, my personal life also encountered serious strains. In 1962, I decided to separate from my wife. Most tragically, our 3-month-old baby died in a crib when a plastic bumper pad smothered her. In 1963, I moved out and established residence in another place but still supported my three children until we were able to make the divorce final and sell our house. All this occurred while I was trying to raise the capital that would help sustain and grow the company.

A very fortunate thing happened to me in 1964, when I took my children on vacation and met an old friend, Shirley Pence, who was also recently separated and was with her children at the same beach resort. One thing led to another, and we were married a year later. We merged our families and looked forward to new, promising lives together — a journey that continues.

In a 1966 trip to New York, I met an investment banker at Paine Webber, who explained to me in meticulous detail the process of going public with a company as small as ours. He said we did not have a chance of going public until we had a gross profit, before taxes, of more than a million dollars. But to make that happen, we had to compound an earnings growth of at least 15 percent a year for five consecutive years and to show that the company could sustain that growth rate. Therefore, I put my long-standing five-year plan to work and charted out what we had to do to accomplish that: how many salesmen we had to hire or recruit on a part-time basis; how many sales they needed to make each month; how much inventory we needed; how much money we could borrow to support all our operations.

The plan worked well. I stayed in touch with the investment bankers each year, sent them regular reports and tried to keep score on everything we were doing. So by 1969, the Paine Webber people said that if we could continue the 15-percent growth for another year, they would take us public in the spring of 1970. By then, we had produced a new catalogue, and sales were booming. Everybody was very upbeat about the company. It seemed that there was an unlimited opportunity to recruit part-time sales people, because everybody wanted to make a little extra money.

In April of 1970, Paine Webber made a national offering of an over-the-counter stock of the Stuart McGuire Company. The stock came out at $12 a share, but almost immediately, the stock market was in trouble. The share price fell two days after the public offering to $10 and then to $9. Sales began to falter, as well as our profits. About that time, shopping centers around the country and the first shopping mall in the Roanoke area opened. Shopping centers generally drew customers through two anchor tenants, usually a grocery store and a department store, but many also had four or five shoe stores. Because so many more shoe outlets opened in the late '60s and early '70s, we had much more local competition.

About the same time, clothing trends changed to the casual market. Our forté had been work shoes for the working man and dress shoes for everybody else. We had a women's shoe division, but it was never tremendously successful. In the door-to-door business, we had a number of obstacles to overcome, because the natural instinct is to ask of a salesman who appears at the door to sell a shoe from a catalogue: "How do I know it will fit?" But we developed a money-back guarantee, and even offered at one point to let people try the shoes for 30 days. If they were not satisfied, they could get a full refund. One of our biggest selling points was that we had a large assortment of sizes and widths, so essentially we could fit anybody, from a men's AA to EEEE, and sometimes up to sizes 16, 17 and 18. Most retail stores really carried only one or two widths. So we developed these exclusive features, which kept the business going for another 15 years.

Among the best pieces of advice from Paine Webber that I accepted was the strong recommendation to operate our new public business under an outside board of directors. One of those directors, Roy Simpson, at each board meeting always asked the question, "Cabell, explain to me what business we're in." And I had the responsibility of explaining each time exactly what that was. This was a wonderful exercise, because in 1971 and 1972, when our sales and profits declined, I had to re-evaluate what business we actually were in. That re-examination led me to understand that we were not just a shoe or clothing business but were more precisely a *distribution* business. If indeed we were in the business of receiving and shipping orders, it didn't make any difference whether it was shoes, and it really didn't make any difference whether it was our business. So to take advantage of our distribution facilities and warehouse that we expanded in 1970, we started a division called MarketTechs, through which we actually solicited business from other mail-order companies, processing their orders. We were one of the first companies in America to do this.

As time went on, we found it more difficult to recruit part-time sales people who would stay with us for any length of time. It became more difficult to compete with the increase in local retail outlets and with the change in the fashion market, since athletic shoes were coming into the picture with Nike, Adidas, Reebok and others. Therefore, our direct selling business declined, but fortunately the MarketTechs distribution business increased.

At the same time, we started our own mail-order companies. From a strategic marketing position, competition between a mail-order company and its catalogue put its sales force in the field at a disadvantage by making salesmen virtually obsolete. We started mail-order companies under different names, with a different line of products but still with a central inventory for the nationwide distribution. This change in our business strategy from exclusively direct selling into mail-order distribution was a transformation that we did not anticipate but that fortunately we were able to adjust to.

Recognizing how to make such adjustments became clearer and easier by taking advantage of the experiences of others, primarily by participating in as many trade associations as possible. I gained significant insights through the Direct Selling Association, as it is called today. I took an early interest in the association, which concentrated on protecting the rights of part-time salesmen as independent contractors, rather than as licensed employees of the companies they represented. I was active in helping to move the organization to Washington, change its name and hire a professional staff so that it could perform the advocacy with Congress so essential to preserve the rights of free-enterprise and part-time, independent contractors. It just celebrated its 100th anniversary as a trade association. I took a similarly active role in the Direct Marketing Association, the trade association for the mail-order industry. Participating in such organizations became critical in building not only individual businesses but also in nurturing contacts that proved invaluable in any number of activities in the future, both commercial and civic.

Hiring and developing the management team and other employees of the business, along with the reorganization around computers and the technology that has kept changing all these years, taught me many lessons about hiring and training people and meeting people's needs.

We were able to set up one of the first pension plans in the Roanoke Valley. We had developed a health plan with the local Blue Cross-Blue Shield company, through which we paid for 50 percent of the cost of health care. We established vacation plans and other benefits so as to meet the needs of the employees in every respect. One of the most important things we were able to do in the mail-order business was to develop a flex-time schedule for working mothers, since most of our employees were women processing orders in the office, and we were able to anticipate reasonably well the workload the day before on the basis of the orders received. We could schedule part-time workers around their own schedules, and they could come to work after they'd put their children in school and leave before the children were out of school. Many employees worked just five or six hours a day. We were able to tailor our work plan and work force to meet the needs of the people, and we enjoyed a great deal of employee loyalty — and consequent customer satisfaction — because we were one of the first companies in our region to implement such an array of benefits.

In other words, doing well by people not only has demonstrable benefits in terms of productivity but the entire enterprise creates a community of interest that, if properly attended to, thrives and prospers. And it's also the right thing to do.

Such convictions in business seemed to me about as self-evident as anything could be, and the same convictions should be no less applicable in any organization within any community.

Looking back over the 38 years I was at the helm of Stuart McGuire before selling it in 1986, the critical constant in achieving so much was realizing the need to become involved locally and nationally in every organization possible. Such involvement allowed me to learn how to create business opportunities, to achieve efficiency and effectiveness in producing whatever product or services are at the heart of any career, and to find or make opportunities available to transfer knowledge and skills to the strengthening of communities at every level.

Lessons learned in my business career were of great benefit when I began to seek ways to give back to the community as part of the commitment I had made to devote 20 percent of my time and effort to building up my community. The federal Economic Opportunity Act of 1964 opened the way to make that contribution, and in subsequent years I have been fortunate to expand the horizons of my own service from the local level to the far reaches of the globe.

As discussed earlier, I had become active in the Salem Rotary Club, the local chamber of commerce and other civic groups. I was asked in the late 1950s to become a member of the Council of Community Services board of directors, which oversaw all of the social programs in the Roanoke Valley, especially those under the United Way. In one meeting in early 1965, a board member made a motion that the council adopt a resolution never to get involved in that "boondoggle" in Washington called the poverty program. I knew instinctively that if that man was against a proposition, I would probably be for it, since I have always been a liberal Democrat and knew him as a conservative Republican. I suggested that we table the motion and study the Economic Opportunity Act of 1964. When I called our congressman, conservative Republican Richard Poff, to ask for copies of the legislation, he said, "Cabell, what do you want copies of that boondoggle legislation for? I voted against it." I said we wanted to study it because it's now the law and we wanted to see how it might help our local area. He replied, "I don't think you want to get involved, but I'll send you the copies." So he did, and I distributed them to the members of the committee and other people in the community, and we studied it carefully.

I was convinced that the law presented an opportunity to local community groups to set up development and social-services programs through which most of the money would come from the federal government. It seemed obvious to me that if these resources were available to us for social programs dedicated to poor people that we should participate. I asked the Council of Community Services board to appoint a committee to examine the opportunities and authorize us to go to the local governments and see if they would participate. I gave copies of the legislation to the council members from the relevant jurisdictions and suggested that they each select members of a panel to study how the region could benefit from the new law. So the board created a 12-person commission, which elected me as chairman.

We eventually committed ourselves to the "business" of reducing poverty. We created a new agency Total Action Against Poverty, or TAP, and our motto was "A hand up, not a handout." We applied strict, prudent business principles of measurable effectiveness and accountability to the organization and administration of the agency.

After a few meetings, I happened to be in Washington on business and dropped by the Office of Economic Opportunity. As luck would have it, I was walking down the hall toward the office when I met the director of the agency, Sargent Shriver, the person I had intended to see. I introduced myself, told him that I was a businessman who happened to be in Washington and that I was chairman of a Virginia local commission considering participation in the poverty program. He invited me into his office. That was the start of a lifelong friendship.

Inside his office, I said, "Mr. Shriver, we're trying to study whether we want to have a community action agency or not." He replied, "There's nothing to study. Just do it. We've got the money, it's already been appropriated. Make an application. We've received only a few of these."

I took the application back to Roanoke and consulted with the other members of the commission. We decided to form a community action agency, which was a coordinated body that would study issues related to the poor and request funds from the federal government to establish programs to mitigate, if not solve, the identified problems. Without much sense of how to proceed, the chairman of the Council of Community Services, Dave Herbert, suggested that the council apply for an $87,000 federal planning grant to hire three people to lead research into areas of need and possible avenues of correcting poverty-related problems in the region. With a deadline facing us, Herbert and I spent all night completing the application. I then made a special trip to Washington to present the proposal to Shriver. He had it approved while I was there. Before I returned, Shriver told me he would like our agency to begin a Head Start program. I had no idea what he was talking about, so he explained that it was an early-childhood intervention to address poverty at its roots. The program provided at least one meal a day and instruction that would give poor pre-school children a "head start" when they were old enough to enter first grade. I followed up on his request, and the local agency sought $187,000 to start three Head Start schools in the Roanoke area.

Within two weeks, the request was approved for the program to begin that summer of 1965, and Bristow Hardin, the new executive director of TAP, flew into action. He called me as chairman of the agency: "Cabell, get the school superintendents together tomorrow night with their superintendents of instruction." I replied, "Bristow, we can't do this tomorrow night. These people have schedules." He repeated, "Get 'em together tomorrow night and tell them we've got money." So I did as Hardin asked, and sure enough the superintendents convened with us. Bristow made a brilliant presentation, saying, "We've got this money. In the summertime, you've got the schools, you've got the teachers. We'll subcontract this program to you. We'll have community groups go out and recruit the students for you. Use your best first grade teachers who would like to be kindergarten teachers, and we'll start this program." Believe it or not, they were able to open in 90 days.

I sensed we were on right path the very first day of Head Start. In Salem, two white twins, 6 years old, appeared from the north side of the city. We served them a meal, and it was hard to believe that those children had not used a knife, fork or spoon. They had eaten only with their hands. It was obvious what the problems were and what we could do to help those children learn and adjust to society. The basic point is that these children and their families were not a part of American society. They were outside of the mainstream. And one of the most important points driven home to us was that poverty was far from a uniquely African-American circumstance. Even today, most of the poor in America are white. As the situation of those two young twins from Salem indicated, the face of poverty in America is not only black, even though the burden certainly falls disproportionately on black American families. According to the U.S. Census Bureau, about 40 percent of those families are regarded as poor. Reducing poverty, especially in this most affluent nation in world history, requires a greater determination to attack it wherever it exists because of poverty's toxic effect on any society where it is allowed to persist.

Early in TAP's existence, the board and key managers understood the value of generating economic activity, even if at a modest level. In 1968, TAP formed the Southwest Virginia Development Corporation, which drew upon grants from the federal Small Business Administration to provide technical assistance to entrepreneurs and small businesses that otherwise would not be able to obtain commercial financing from a bank. Some of those funds then were devoted to hiring people with few skills but in need of entering the work force. In addition, job training for those workers would supplement the grants to the small businesses to encourage the infrastructure to nurture and sustain local economic growth. TAP also initiated a micro-enterprise lending program, which has grown and continues even today, allowing people without extensive credit histories to open very small businesses from scratch. Twenty years after beginning the Southwest Virginia Development Corporation, I realized that TAP was definitely on the right track. I had gone to Bangladesh on a volunteer assignment for the United Nations in 1989, and again with my wife, Shirley, in 1990. While there, and on other occasions later, I exchanged ideas with Muhammad Yunus, the founder of the Grameen Bank, which had begun micro-enterprise lending on the other side of the world. Grameen now serves small entrepreneurs in 125 countries, an achievement that earned Yunus the 2006 Nobel Peace Prize because of his work to help people go to work and end poverty.

One of the least understood problems in society is the effect of releasing ex-offenders from prison without adequate preparation for re-entry to the "world outside." At TAP, we recognized that Virginia traditionally released prisoners with nothing more than a modest amount of cash, a bus ticket and the contact information for a parole officer. Someone who has been confined in prison for 10 or 20 years and is out of touch with society — and perhaps unwelcome by family members — and with no place else to go, may return to the streets and a continued life of crime unless provided transitional preparation, including job skills. TAP noted the need for creating a means for that transition and began its TAP Offender Program in 1975. Within three years, the concept was sufficiently attractive that several other Virginia community action agencies formed a statewide network under the umbrella program, Virginia Community Action Reentry System, or Virginia CARES. The program was carefully developed on a test basis with a grant from the Ford Foundation to counsel prisoners before their release and to prepare them to be reintegrated into the community. When released, they would have a place to go when they got off the bus, and they would receive further job training. This program has demonstrated the potential reduction of recidivism by more than 50 percent, and is extremely cost-effective. But the prevailing attitude among so many leaders in the country today, as it has been for the last 25 or 30 years, has been to lock them up, throw away the key and forget about them. It's been very difficult to keep the funds flowing to keep Virginia CARES in business. As the program developed, we learned that many businesses had restrictions on their insurance policies that prevented hiring convicted felons, even though they'd paid their debt to society and were back in the community. In time, we were able to convince local businesses and even their insurance companies to change that rule by sending a Virginia CARES representative to the employer with assurances that the ex-offender had completed the program and was to be trusted. The key has been convincing the potential employers of the importance of creating partnerships to convert the offenders from their old, destructive ways into productive, contributing members of society. Yet the fight to obtain the necessary funding for such an obviously positive program continues in earnest, as it must, against misguided political resistance.

In addition to Head Start, we formed many local committees and neighborhood groups to learn first-hand the nature of poverty and why people were poor, how they lived and what could be done about it. Accordingly, over the next 15 years, TAP developed more than 40 different programs, using the business principle of market segmentation and developing specially trained people and programs to meet the different causes of people's poverty, whether it was lack of education, health, job training, lack of indoor plumbing, adjustment problems for ex-offenders or other barriers that prevented people from supporting themselves. The source of their difficulties may have been as simple as lack of transportation, a phone or basic knowledge of opportunities. In the final analysis, they were not participating in their society. They had no real stake in its vitality and prosperity, and we at TAP decided to help them do everything possible to acquire that stake.

This is not to say that all programs were successful. We experimented with many initiatives that we discontinued because they were impractical or we couldn't get adequate funding.

From my experience in developing a small shoe company, growing its size and product lines through difficult market transitions and nurturing it into a publicly traded company with a global reach, I learned much about the need to keep any organization adaptive, responsive to new conditions and resilient enough to withstand a range of economic and social forces. By the early 1970s, the attraction of foreign labor markets for such products as shoes had begun to exert growing pressure in response to rising costs and narrowing profit margins. I am very sensitive to the consequences of major shifts currently in labor markets that are playing havoc with so many older U.S. manufacturing jobs. I understand from the business executive's perspective as one who had to balance the return on shareholders' investments with the welfare of U.S. shoemakers, which was becoming increasingly automated in the United States anyway.

After contracting with Italian, Spanish and Brazilian manufacturers, I was among the first American businessmen to approach China for negotiations in 1974 to produce our shoes in Chinese factories. This was before the United States established diplomatic relations with the People's Republic of China, so a Canadian trading partner accompanied my wife and me to Shanghai. I had taken some of the patterns and dies from our best-selling Italian-made shoe lines to determine whether the Chinese could produce to our specifications. The workers turned out the samples quickly, so we were encouraged. We placed an order for 40,000 pairs of shoes, which the Chinese promised to fill within 90 days. The shoes finally arrived at our U.S. warehouse a year and a half later, because the primitive state of Chinese industry had no raw materials inventory. They had to make from scratch the thread, nails, soles, heels and other components before assembling the completed shoes. Consequently, our company learned an important, painful lesson. For the Chinese, however, the lesson also was priceless: Learning quickly from such early failures, that growing power in international trade today places great pressure on U.S. manufacturing industries and their U.S. workers.

One of the most critical needs for the U.S. economy will be to retrain workers whose former jobs have either been moved overseas or have become obsolete in the modern economy. That challenge is not new, only more compelling.

TAP recognized how important providing such training can be to keep people fully and productively employed in meaningful, well-paying jobs. That pressure is returning with a vengeance to the

American economy, and the challenge today will be greater than the transitions we faced nearly 40 years ago. One model that could be adapted would be the old Opportunities Industrialization Centers founded in Philadelphia by the Rev. Leon Sullivan, who placed intense emphasis on completing high school and accelerating job training. TAP brought the OIC to Roanoke in the 1970s, and variations on job-training continue through the community action agency for the poor who qualify. Yet beyond just the poor, community colleges today are providing wonderful options for young men and women who seek training for their first career jobs. As more experienced workers begin to see less demand for the skills they may have relied on for several years, society should intensify the programs that will help men and women take advantage of new skills and disciplines. Such training must accelerate, beginning at the local level but coordinated into systematic successes nationwide. That will be a huge organizational and funding challenge in today's climate of skepticism, but one that should stir people to action when they realize that flinching from a national commitment to economic opportunity and justice is in no one's interest in the face of such transformative competitive changes being brought to the world scene by such foreign powers as China, India and Brazil.

In spite of the struggle to keep people's attention focused on meeting the needs of society's unfortunate ones, and on the broad, often unseen consequences for the general welfare when they're allowed to fester, community action agencies are among the most innovative and significant inventions of the 20th century. Figuring out how to leverage money, develop a cash-flow procedure, knowing how to hire and train people to deal with cultural as well as programmatic difficulties were made much easier because of my business experience. In fact, every experience I've had in life in some way came to further fruition and of benefit in this huge new undertaking at TAP.

But there is no substitute for basic, one-on-one human interaction in trying to understand and appreciate other people's difficulties. I recall the time that my wife, Shirley, and I called on a low-income house and a man came to the front door. I asked him whether he was working, and he shook his head. I realized in a few minutes that he wasn't talking. I had learned how to knock on doors from my shoe business, so I was very courteous, knocking on the door, stepping back two steps and of course trying not to intrude on his privacy. But as we continued to talk, I noticed that the man didn't have any teeth. I asked him whether he'd like to have teeth, and he said he couldn't afford them. I knew that the state health department would give dentures to low-income people as a public service. So we arranged transportation for him to go to a clinic, where he eventually was fitted with a new set of teeth. In a short time, his dignity restored, he went to work in a new job, which put him back into society. That's a classic example of how public programs, paid by taxpayers, can become cost-effective.

In another example of personal contact from the early 1970s, Shirley and I had hired a woman who came occasionally to help with a variety of chores with the children. In driving her home one night, we realized that she lived in Roanoke County about 100 yards from the city of Roanoke boundary line. She did not have running water in her house. In Virginia, cities are required to provide water but rural areas are not. That small community of black people just across the line did not have indoor toilets or running water. About that time, one of the committees associated with TAP had begun recognizing similar problems arising from a lack of drinking water and indoor toilets throughout the region. So we put together a proposal to establish a demonstration water project. We were unable to obtain approval for federal funding, so we went to the Ford Foundation, which gave us the initial demonstration grant that proved very successful. We installed three water systems within the first year. The benefits became evident immediately: Economic development escalates with the construction of water systems and roads, with housing following soon after. Thus can a once-desolate community become transformed into one that thrives and allows its residents to become more fully a part of society. And from that first series of projects, the Demonstration Water Project has expanded into a program of national scope.

My experience from TAP has convinced me that all people want a better life for themselves, and especially for their children. All they need is an opportunity. I also learned that race should be absolutely irrelevant, that ethnic origin should be irrelevant. There's a hidden potential in low-income people if we can just open that opportunity to them.

After more than 40 years, we have learned how to solve poverty, which is still generally misunderstood by most of the public, thanks to concerted political efforts to diminish public emphasis on the problem. Equally misunderstood is the value of investing in the abilities of children and adults, investments that pay off in just a few years if they're afforded the chance to master new skills and increasingly contribute to the social and economic life of their communities. Tragically, poverty today around the world is reversing progress and diminishing hope that a globalized economy would improve lives in the developing world. Rising food and energy prices now suggest that the sense of economic equity once promised has slowly been surrendered to forces more inclined toward concentration of wealth than its advocates advertised. Disparities in the allocation of wealth even within the United States the last two decades raise serious questions as to whether economic opportunity and justice are threatened.

This disparity between the increasing gap between the rich and the poor unfortunately is widening, and it manifests itself not just in our society but globally, between rich countries and poor countries.

But there are serious questions now in our society about whether sufficient jobs indeed exist for people who are trained. We've lost most of the manufacturing industry in this country: shoes, garments, textiles, furniture, and even many sectors of the automobile industry. Some people have written that America no longer is the land of opportunity because of the high rate of unemployment and the higher rate of underemployment.

It is time to re-examine the current arms-length role of government as a mediator in the job-creating sector of America's national economy. For more than a century — at least since the "trust-busting" era of Theodore Roosevelt — the United States has relied on a significant role of the federal government to sustain the legitimacy and the integrity of capitalism in its service of this democratic republic. With the election of Ronald Reagan, that stewardship has undergone persistent attack. Deregulatory zeal reached its most permissive status under President George W. Bush, whose administration presided over the greatest economic threat to the nation since the Great Depression.

As history has demonstrated with painful clarity, freeing capital markets to self-regulate invites catastrophe. The nation has had to learn that lesson repeatedly — with the Great Depression, in the savings and loan bailouts of the 1980s, in the bursting of the high-tech bubble in the late 1990s, and of course in the housing debacle fed by a virtually unregulated financial sector gone mad. Repeatedly in modern American history, the federal government has been a reliable guarantor of the nation's economic dynamism, but only because of its legitimacy as the sole source of democratic mediation in the economy under the rule of law. Markets and financial sectors left to operate beyond the rule of law invite the destructive chaos the country experiences when it "forgets" the lessons of history. Markets exist, after all, to serve society, not the other way around.

The extent of the federal government's role in actually creating jobs is debatable in this democracy — whether from enacting job-creating tax incentives, to merely "jawboning" industries into hiring workers or to acting as the provider of guaranteed employment — but no reasonable person with a working knowledge of history can escape realizing the need for commitment to a more assertive role by the federal government in seeing to it that all who wish to work will have productive employment worthy of their talents and human dignity.

As he so often did, Franklin D. Roosevelt articulated for future generations the ideals of a great, just and noble nation. He exhorted his fellow Americans to embrace the future vigorously — together.

"Full employment means not only jobs — but productive jobs," Roosevelt said as the end of World War II began to come into view. He knew the importance of retaining the vigor of the work force that had endured throughout the war. "Americans do not regard jobs that pay substandard wages as productive jobs. We must make sure that private enterprise works as it is supposed to work — on the basis of initiative and vigorous competition, without the stifling presence of monopolies and cartels."

Now a decade into the 21st century, renewed concentration of massive industries threatens the strangulating consequences of monopoly power in too many sectors of the global economy, including the United States. Such concentration poses a genuine hazard that should arouse the interest and determination of every citizen to become involved in understanding the perils of economic concentration to the economic well-being of all American workers. Every concerned American should become active in demanding that elected representatives safeguard the dynamism and resilience of economic institutions through enlightened regulation.

As I write, the country still suffers from extraordinarily high unemployment — more than 9 percent. Questions have been raised as to whether indeed there are enough jobs in this country for our growing population. Over the past decade, essentially no new jobs have been created. This means we have the same number of jobs in our economy as 10 years ago with a significant increase in population. All of this is having a devastating effect on the struggling sectors where the unemployment rate is more than twice as high. Defining more clearly and assertively the role of government to mediate these destructive distortions in our national economy — and the lives of our fellow Americans — strikes me as everyone's duty and a civic action truly in the national interest.

Two major experiences in my life — building a business and organizing a community action agency — happened concurrently over a 10-year period. It increased, of course, my time commitments, but that taught me how to manage the time with the help of other people to get both jobs done. In those two major endeavors, I learned something essential about human nature: Everyone seeks a better life. This is the fundamental motivation for improving public education and making sure that everyone has the equivalent of a high school education and other specialized training to compete with the jobs in the world. An essential component of this is the integration of our society, recognizing that race should be absolutely irrelevant. We also must make the investments necessary to reverse the resurgence of poverty, which discourages people from participating in society and thus from supporting themselves successfully. Failure to encourage and enable people to become involved in our national life weakens the foundations of a just society.

In my experience, the most ambitious, financially successful, civically involved and publicly respected people have sought not only to make an excellent living but also to make an excellent life. That is achieved primarily by devoting themselves — their time, energy and material resources — to improving the world around them, beginning with their own local communities. I have been fortunate to take advantage of opportunities to combine my business experiences with insights drawn from observing how the Marshall Plan and other investments in society have brought great benefits and remarkable cost-effective payoffs. Conversely, I learned the value of drawing upon my experience in working with non-profit agencies and applying those insights to the effective operation of a business. All of these investments help to strengthen our society. The basic lesson in all of this is to get involved locally with your own family, your own business opportunity, your own community and local organizations. Recognize investment opportunities and apply personal commitment to expanding economic opportunity and social justice in ways that reaffirm the principles of true freedom for all, as embodied in our Constitution.

Chapter Three

Education: Sharing Knowledge and Wisdom

My fellow Virginian, Thomas Jefferson, wrote wisely in 1816, "If a nation expects to be ignorant and free, in a state of civilization, it expects what never was and never will be."

Those stirring words should cause every American concerned about the future of the republic to take note and assess the status of this country's commitment to educating its young people, which will be so essential to preserving the heritage passed to us by our forebears.

Learning begins at birth and continues throughout life, not necessarily limited to a formal school setting. But formal education marks the fundamental difference between successful, forward thinking societies and those in developing countries. The single greatest difference is public education.

Education is much more complicated in our post-industrial, information-era world than it was when I was growing up. If people are going to compete successfully for the higher-paying jobs in the global economy, they will have to learn more about so many different subjects than in previous generations. The general perception that a 12-year course of study provides a sufficient "education" is no longer adequate.

I grew up in a family and in a local culture that took basic education for granted, although I never experienced formal early-childhood preparation such as kindergarten. Even so, I was always blessed with the desire to learn, taking extra courses at every opportunity, including participation on the high school newspaper, the yearbook and debate team. The decision to attend college was easy for me. My father, an alumnus of Virginia Military Institute, never allowed me to consider going anywhere else but VMI. Later, with the Army during World War II, I was amazed by how a sophisticated society such as the German people could be so brainwashed by Hitler that they would further the Nazi cause.

People who are proud of the American pre-eminence from the victory in World War II through the amazing discoveries leading to the space program and to almost incredible advances in medical and other fields of science should be astounded by the fact that the United States has one of the highest dropout rates in the industrialized world. Our students go to school less than the students in most of the developed nations. U.S. education today pays for about 13 years of public schooling for nine months a year. In Japan, the school year is 11 months, which is almost a third more schooling for a student's formal educational experience. Where I live in Southwest Virginia, 30 percent of the adults do not have a high school education. In Roanoke, 57 percent of the high school freshmen drop out before they graduate. Every year, an estimated 1 million high school students nationwide drop out of high school — about one every 26 seconds, according to a computation by *New York Times* columnist Bob Herbert. The United States is falling behind in preparing its people to compete successfully for the meaningful, satisfying, well-paying jobs in the current and future global economy, and too many of our young people grow into adulthood without the historical understanding and commitment to civic discipline that are every American's responsibility as well as birthright.

Of all the disputes that I've had in all my years of trying to raise funds for our community action agency and other programs, the one social investment that I have found to inspire unanimous agreement has been acceptance of the essential need to educate our children. Everyone agrees it's critical, but no one knows exactly how to pay for it adequately. Far too many are unwilling to pay the necessary price for it. What, then, is the role of government in ensuring that people in educationally deficient areas qualify for the jobs of today and have the opportunity to reach their own personal potential? One critical consideration increasingly and repeatedly persists: *how* to pay for public schools, because most of the problems involve adequate financing. Expecting local governments to cover the full cost is unrealistic. Those jurisdictions, which already pay for about 50 percent or 60 percent of the public schools in their areas, rely too much on real estate taxes instead of general revenue — a fiscal conundrum that will persist until the public decides to adopt a rational tax system that tracks the actual economy and not some antiquated tax practices from the nation's agrarian past.

But that is another public policy topic, and in the meantime, too many politicians continue to exert pressure on educators to experiment with new, buck-passing fads, the latest being No Child Left Behind, ill-named because so many are indeed being left behind. According to the Bill and Melinda Gates Foundation, which financed a nationwide study of the U.S. public education system, a third of the students nationwide drop out of high school. Another third are not prepared either to perform productive work or college-level education. Two-thirds, in effect, are indeed being left behind to a certain extent. As Bill Gates said a few years ago in a scathing critique of the current secondary school system, which he called "obsolete": "When I compare our high schools with what I see when I'm traveling abroad, I am terrified for our work force of tomorrow. By obsolete, I don't just mean that they are broken, flawed or under-funded, though a case could be made for every one of those points. By obsolete, I mean our high schools — even when they're working as designed — cannot teach all our students what they need to know today."

A 2007 report from the Educational Testing Service, "America's Perfect Storm," warned of three major trends that may threaten the future quality of life for millions of Americans. First is the wide disparity in the literacy and math skills of both those of school age and adults. Such skills vary widely across racial, ethnic and socioeconomic groups. Second, the global economy has forced massive changes in the U.S. economy, especially through technological changes and a radical shift in the relationship of labor and capital. Finally, the nation is experiencing vast demographic changes, with the U.S. population expected to reach 360 million by 2030. Immigration as well as an aging work force will accelerate the anticipated dislocations for workers already experiencing difficulty in entering the high-tech and information-age careers of the future.

As a parent and a grandparent with 13 grandchildren, I would like for each one of my grandchildren to learn how to be extraordinary. I think every parent and grandparent would like the same thing. Yet the nation has been erratic in providing the educational opportunity necessary to reverse the trends that suggest ominous futures for so many Americans.

Every college graduate, every citizen, every person in any career in the United States should devote a portion of his or her life to dealing with the educational system. In the opening chapter, I asked: *"If Not Me, Then Who?"* Who is going to solve this problem, and how is it going to be solved? The fact is, it can be solved only with the active involvement of everyone in this country, particularly the parents of children. All parents want a better life for their children. The American dream was based on building a better life for subsequent generations. In this country today, we're doing just the opposite. Should we continue along this misdirected course, our country will not be the global powerhouse in the next generation that it is today. Our children are not being prepared for the best jobs by the evolving global economy, nor are we leaving the country in better shape environmentally for our children.

I note emphatically that the problems of school dropouts and other weaknesses in our educational system are not entirely the responsibility of the schools themselves. A large part of the problem, particularly in the lower-income, center-city schools is rooted in the family, in poverty itself, in the lack of participation by disadvantaged people, and ultimately in children who grow up with no hope.

Many of the schools in the United States are first-class for what they do in the number of days that the children are in school. But 30 percent or more who simply fail to meet this test reflects a systemic cycle of failure of fearsome proportions. These are the schools in urban and rural communities with high concentrations of low-income children. The youngsters are just as inherently capable of being great scientists, doctors and executives as suburban children, but most of those low-income schools in America are simply bad, not only denying the children who attend them the equal opportunity that is their right but squandering about a third of our intellectual capital. To put this point in simple terms, the choice these urban center-city disadvantaged children have is to be motivated either to be successful in school or turn to drugs and guns. Then everyone loses.

Unfortunately, our nation faces this serious problem at more than one level. Too many — at least one-third, according to the findings of the Educational Testing Service — are nearing adulthood and stand precariously at the threshold of careers that, for better or worse, they are ill-prepared to undertake. They lack the necessary basic skills for the world of work to provide for themselves, much less a family. Soon the dropouts and others who are ill-prepared for the workplace will join the ranks of older workers who already are finding a cruel reality confronting them as globalization and modernization diminish the value of their already limited job skills. Those older workers have not received the new or upgraded training that they, and the American economy, need to contribute to a more vibrant, growing and self-reliant society. Such conditions pose the threat that, if not corrected, a significant portion of the population eventually will become alienated and begin to lose the critical sense of owning a stake in the success of the American experiment. If only as a practical matter, that is a dangerous path for any democratic republic to approach.

I am convinced that the greatest challenge before the United States today is the massive work yet to be done in preparing all our people to build and advance our society. We can, if we choose to do so, draw on some experiences of the past that began to move the nation in the right direction but that somehow suffered from lost confidence and blurred vision by too many American political leaders. We continue to pay a terrible price for having lost our way.

Probably the most far-reaching and successful endeavor to advance comprehensive public education came with the federal Head Start program. By 1965, Head Start was among the earliest programs of Total Action Against Poverty, the community action agency in Roanoke. Head Start was part of the Johnson administration's so-called war on poverty and focused intently on early-childhood education. I also learned first-hand a great deal from my wife, Shirley, who was a pre-school teacher for 18 years. Her experience and counsel impressed on me the importance of early learning, with loving and caring parents as well as learning from peers and broader community reinforcement of learning at the earliest possible age. The key to Head Start was to take disadvantaged, low-income children and their parents and introduce them to formal learning so that when they entered the first grade they would not fall behind and eventually drop out. One of the most valuable aspects of our Head Start program was the parents' councils that provided feedback and open lines of communication in the teaching and learning process, which in time could become reinforced throughout the "network" connecting teacher, student, parent and even entire neighborhoods where the families lived. Childhood immunizations and regular health care as needed from the earliest possible age also contributed to the care for all aspects of the child's development. Furthermore, among the most compelling strengths of Head Start has been the extraordinary influence of children learning from their peers. Our experience at TAP has convinced me that the variety of their backgrounds — particularly when the program was occasionally able to draw from a wide demographic cross section of society — contributed to a phenomenal stimulation of the learning process. That same concept or some adaptation, I am convinced, remains just as crucial today, if not more so. Yet the lackluster commitment of most states to supplement the relatively modest federal funding for the program has compromised the promising outcomes Head Start could achieve. Each generation should accept the responsibility to keep faith with all members of our society in providing equal opportunity for an education that will help break the cycles of ignorance and poverty.

History reminds us of the injustices of slavery and, especially in the South where I grew up, the evils of legal segregation, which denied millions of Americans opportunities that were rightly theirs. Living as I did in that span from 1950 to 1970 when Virginia closed down black schools and the courts resorted to compulsory busing, I began to ask myself about America's role as a model of its professed values in the modern industrial world. My wife and I journeyed to Australia and arranged to spend time in a village deep into Arnheim Land to see how the Aborigines lived and coped, especially in view of the Western education system the British were trying to introduce to the Aborigine society. We also visited a village in Botswana, staying there several days with the Bushmen and observing other indigenous societies such as the Masai tribe in East Africa. The essential lesson we learned about those cultures was that each child learned the basic skills of survival. All children had to be educated to learn to live within their environment and sustain themselves with the resources that were available.

Universal application of that fundamental insight became inescapable in the work I have been able to do with the National Academy of Sciences as a member of its President's Circle and with other organizations that deal with education. Globalization has contributed to the "creative destruction" of many well-paying jobs in America and the emergence of technological demands for entirely new skills. The academy's 2007 report, *Rising Above the Gathering Storm: Energizing and Employing America for a Brighter Economic Future*, emphasizes dramatically the need to have more advanced science and math preparation in our public schools and through college to qualify for the jobs of the future. As a case in point, I recall a National Academies meeting at Stanford University just a few years ago, when I asked Craig Barrett, the chairman of Intel, whether his company would have more jobs in the United States in the next five years than they have now. He said, yes, a few, but many more overseas. The reason he gave was that in his industry, he can hire five engineers in India and China for the same price that he has to pay one American, and on the average, the Indian and Chinese employee is better qualified for his type of work. As I noted earlier, this offers hard evidence of the lack of an emphasis on science and math in our educational system.

This is not to imply that the Indians and Chinese are brighter. It just means their brightest students have been educated better than our merely above-average or average students, and of course we have to realize that the engineers that a company like Intel would hire represent the top 5 percent of the students in those foreign countries. Not all of the graduates of the schools in China and India could compete at the same level, but their best ones do.

Despite its unfortunate financial struggles in the last several years, the Head Start program has proved that low-income children, when they start in a structured learning environment by age 4, are better prepared by far than those low-income children who have not been through Head Start. There's a lower dropout rate and a higher achievement level. This is a program that could help mitigate the poverty problem significantly in the United States if it were fully funded, and if local and state governments would step up and match the federal investment to extend its services to all children. In other words, the public education system in this country needs to be expanded to 14 years with more year-round schools. All children should receive guaranteed health care and pre-school opportunities. The only way to implement this is through local initiative, with local inspirational leaders coming forth to insist that legislatures and school boards take action.

In our local TAP program, we recognized early that people were poor because they don't support themselves, or participate in society, and the only way to encourage and attract them into the mainstream of the community is to help them acquire the skills so that they can have better jobs that allow them to support themselves and their families. Head Start was the first such effort for TAP, followed in 1978 with the anti-school dropout program Project Discovery, which encourages low-income and particularly black students to get through high school and plan to attend college. We started the first general equivalency diploma (GED) program in our valley outside the public schools. Now through technology, there's an opportunity with digital television, particularly with public television, to have ongoing GED programs and other educational programs for all adults, such as the 30 percent in our region who do not have a high school education.

Forward-looking former Governor Timothy Kaine was among the most energetic proponents of early-childhood education in an era when most public officials have been more sensitive to prevailing winds of anti-tax sentiment than investment in the future of the nation's children, and by extension the nation's social and economic progress. Unfortunately, Governor Kaine's successor, Bob McDonnell, and the Virginia General Assembly have been less enlightened in their willingness to provide the full level of resources to implement these proposals.

Kaine sponsored his Smart Beginnings Summit in the summer of 2006 to advance his proposed policy objective of providing early-childhood development through pre-kindergarten for all Virginia 4-year-olds. Research shows that investing early in a child's life results in improved labor productivity, competitiveness, economic growth and job creation for the population as a whole. Scientific studies indicate that 85 percent of the brain's capacity is in place by age 5, so the first years of life are the most critical in contributing to healthy social and intellectual growth and development. As we learned as long ago as 1965 in our Head Start program, investing in parents and children early builds a strong foundation that reinforces later cognitive and social capabilities, school achievement and ultimately life success. In addition, economic projections indicate that $1 invested in high-quality early-childhood education can yield as much as $9 in future savings from forgone social services and lower crime rates and rates of incarceration. Children with good early-learning opportunities have fewer special education needs in later years, tend to score higher on math and science achievement tests and are more likely to graduate from high school. They are more likely to go on to pursue higher levels of education, to earn more money and consequently pay more in state and federal taxes, thus reversing dependence on such sources for income assistance.

Getting involved with advocating such programs strikes me as a self-evident responsibility for any citizen who cares about the future, but elected officials need the participation of more and more concerned citizens. If I could give one piece of advice to any such concerned citizen — but especially parents — it would be to get involved with the local school board and to bring increased local interest, commitment and pressure to improve, at least gradually, the local school system. In turn, that pressure should force the attention upward, toward state officials, to make the changes and the necessary investment in all our children's development.

Success in opening wider avenues to higher-quality education will not be measured by "educational" solutions alone, that is, merely on such indices as teacher salaries, classroom space, textbooks and school budgets. Schools are part of a larger community, and they function only as well as the wider community where they do their work. This lesson became painfully clear to me a few years ago when, as part of a tour sponsored by the National Academies, I visited school systems in Washington, D.C., New York City and San Francisco. In each of those three districts, I asked the superintendents whether they worked with the local community action agency and the other similar local entities in the community to help them with the school dropout problem. I received the same answer everywhere: No, they didn't work with them. That's a big mistake. I learned from Head Start and other TAP programs that there are skilled people in all the 1,000 community action agencies across the United States who can help the public schools with their dropout program and other initiatives targeted directly and indirectly to help children stay in school.

Recently in Roanoke, the new school superintendent called a meeting with the head of our local community college system and our local TAP community action agency to see how the institutions could work together toward that end. Such collaboration will pay off as time goes by, because the community college system has the best vocational education program around. The combination of community organizations can help bring hope to those in the low-income community, and specifically to the children.

I don't mean to imply that there haven't been some well-intentioned efforts, even with the misguided No Child Left Behind, which was never properly funded, and the idea of vouchers, charter schools, governor's schools, gifted student programs and the nationwide emphasis on standardized testing. But the net result has been no improvement in the last 15 or 20 years in the achievement levels of 17-year-olds in our public school system in math, science and reading. That fact alone is the best example that I can give for everyone in our society to become involved in some way to help educate our children so that they can qualify for the jobs of the future.

Perhaps the most gratifying source of my hope for a brighter education future has been the dedication of college students who already have benefited personally from their own academic achievements. I have been heartened by witnessing a surge the last several years in young people's awakening to the obstacles that poverty can raise not only for poor people but for the society that forfeits access to the talents and abilities of those unable to achieve the promise of educational opportunity.

When I sold the Stuart McGuire Company in 1986, the president of Roanoke College, Dr. Norman Fintel, called me and asked me to lunch. "Cabell, I see that you've sold your business, and I know what you've been doing with TAP and other programs in the valley, and I want to offer you an office to continue this work." That afternoon, he drove me around the Elizabeth campus, which the college had recently purchased in an area of Salem apart from the main campus. He said, "We have an empty building here, so why don't you take it, fix it up and have an office and start a center for our college, a center dedicated to whatever discipline, program or other activity that we're not doing at the college and something you think our students need to learn." That was perhaps the greatest compliment that anyone ever paid me.

I accepted Dr. Fintel's invitation by establishing a center for research and public discourse on critical topics related primarily to poverty, the environment and peace. In 1988, the Cabell Brand Center for International Poverty and Resource Studies opened on the Elizabeth Campus of Roanoke College. For 18 years, the center hosted conferences and symposiums, but the greatest contribution, I believe, was the center's opening to students from all the local regional colleges challenging opportunities to qualify for grants to study poverty and environmental issues. Grants of between $500 and $1,000 were underwritten by contributions from more than 60 local businesses and individuals who were willing to support the student fellowships. Our fund-raising activities emphasized that we use other revenue to pay for the operating costs of the center, but all the local contributions went to the students. This was an appealing way to involve students in using "real-world" problems of poverty and environmental deterioration as laboratories not only to understand the nature of those issues but also to inspire the students to seek solutions. In that way, their education through research and a published research paper enriched their own learning and also contributed further to the education of the local community that helped to support it. In essence, the center viewed its mission as drawing young, local minds to examine such global concerns as avenues to guide societies to implement economic, political and social systems that enable people to support themselves materially, live peacefully, protect human values and sustain environmental health in the process. The center's focus for the students always was to concentrate on initiatives that would benefit the local area while maintaining a national and global perspective. In all, the center awarded more than 500 fellowships, all bestowed with the ultimate objective of planting in each student's mind the question that is fundamental to any free and just society: "How can we in this generation leave the world better than we found it?"

Young people, I am convinced, have always been the source of every older generation's hope. The duty of the older generations is to inspire and urge those who follow them to advance the best cultural, economic, political and environmental causes they have inherited. Understanding their society, in all its complexity and even its contradictions, should be a civic value that becomes part of every young person's overall education and practical preparation for his or her personal and community lives. Such motives guided my desire to establish the Cabell Brand Center.

Such ideals, I firmly believe, have never been more capably expressed — and indeed achieved — than in the Shepherd Program for the Interdisciplinary Study of Poverty and Human Capability at Washington and Lee University in Lexington, Virginia. Since its formation in 1997, the Shepherd Program has integrated academic study and learning through service and reflection, seeking to inform students about poverty and what can be done to foster human capabilities for communities and individuals who have been left behind in domestic and international development.

Just after the Shepherd Program was officially inaugurated, I was invited to lunch by Howard Packett, an old friend and business associate of mine from Salem, as well as a Washington and Lee alumnus. We joined Harlan Beckley, a visionary W&L professor who as the program founder remains its director, and Tom Shepherd, an alumnus who had contributed a substantial amount of money to begin a program at the university to study poverty. I was invited because of the role I had played in helping to organize TAP, the regional community action agency with its dozens of programs designed to reduce poverty. Lexington is in Rockbridge County, which is part of the region served by TAP in Southwest Virginia. The lunch was intended to explore possible partnerships and evaluate how best to combine theoretical inquiry of the academic world with the practical world of delivering social services.

I had never met Harlan Beckley and Tom Shepherd before, but they immediately told me the story of why Washington and Lee was starting the Shepherd Poverty Program. I began to think of what Dr. Norm Fintel had asked me to do at Roanoke College and also what

Sargent Shriver had told me about the long-term solution for poverty, starting with children. So I arranged for Beckley and Shepherd to visit TAP, starting with the Head Start program and then the other job-training programs. That series of visits helped to create the momentum for the structuring of an academic and practical approach first conceived by several members of the university faculty who had concluded a few years before that Washington and Lee students tended to be insulated by their relative affluence and privilege. As a result, they had virtually no knowledge or understanding of the "real world" of poverty in the sense that a fully educated person should have. The professors brainstormed the prospect of forming interdisciplinary courses and a variety of practical experiences for students to expose them to the problems within society. They presented their proposal to the university President John Elrod, who was impressed and responded favorably. Elrod approached Shepherd for financial support, and the groundwork for the program began.

I had been invited to that lunch with Harlan Beckley and Tom Shepherd primarily because I was still the chairman of TAP. That connection is critically important to illustrate the underlying thesis of this book: Because of the extensive work of TAP and the ensuing publicity through the news media, the professors who were conceiving a program for their students to understand the causes and effects of poverty were familiar with the programs provided by TAP. Those included Head Start, job-training, the homeless shelter, the food bank, ex-offender re-entry services and a host of educational initiatives. They saw the potential in possible laboratory experiences and internships. Washington and Lee, with Shepherd's financial "jump-start," eventually led to the program's initial courses in the fall of 1997. Since that lunch, I have been fortunate to act in a number of ways to expand the offerings to students. I have talked with classes, offered suggestions on course subjects and proposed other ways that the program might be improved.

For more than a decade, the Shepherd Program has offered courses and made available internships to Washington and Lee students. Among the earliest such opportunities were summer service projects for students at various TAP programs. With that model, and not content to sit on their laurels, the faculty and staff of the program have expanded the concept to form the Shepherd Alliance, which places as many as 60 students from Washington and Lee, Berea College, Middlebury College, Morehouse College, Spelman College and participating Bonner Scholar institutions in two-month, full-time summer internships with non-profit agencies in the eastern United States. Through private donations, the Shepherd Program has been expanded to Baylor, Rice, and Furman University. Now, seeking even brighter horizons under Harlan Beckley's leadership as founder and director, the Shepherd Program has proposed an even bolder initiative. Today, one-third of Washington and Lee students, including those in the law school, take courses and involve themselves in some way in the programs designed to redress poverty. Some students have become so involved that they have focused their life goals to pursue public service as a vital part of their careers.

Congress has authorized in the higher education bill a provision to combine the existing Shepherd Alliance with other significant universities to produce an 11-school, five-year project for the study of poverty and human capability — the first of its kind in undergraduate education. The Shepherd Consortium will add to the current alliance Georgetown University, Notre Dame University, Morgan State University, the University of Arkansas at Little Rock, the University of Richmond, and Vanderbilt University.

The point here, as has been the case so many times in my life, is that by seizing one opportunity after another, each series of relationships acquired continues to open new doors to new opportunities for service. By getting involved with the local community yet thinking globally, one thing keeps leading to another.

From the beginning of the learning continuum in the first four years through the highest levels of graduate school, the most extensive education possible for each individual determines not only each person's "success" in life but also the strength, resilience and fairness of our entire society. Unfortunately, the promise of that equal opportunity to the fullest possible education has not rung true for too many Americans. Unless the American people insist on a course correction to restore credibility to that promise, it will ring all the more hollow.

Each of us should seize the opportunity to participate in some way with educational institutions, whether with the school board, on an advisory committee, in speaking to classes, meeting with students and encouraging local officials and legislators to put a primary focus of their resource allocation on education. We all want our children and grandchildren to reach their full potential and have as much education as possible. This is a local issue and it's a global issue. To do this, we need more effective, robust, comprehensive standards to measure achievement. Being content with political phrases such as "No Child Left Behind" should no longer be acceptable. We need enormous resources to attract the best-qualified people to be the teachers, curriculum developers and administrators in all school systems.

We're discovering that education is much more than learning the content of books and mastering new technologies. We realize that the highly educated person, the person who really is enjoying life and fulfilling his or her potential, requires development of all the human capacities. We should encourage our children to realize that education never stops. We — and eventually they — must continue to learn how to solve the complex array of problems facing us, such as the environmental issues of global climate change and its potential to endanger the very survival of the planet itself.

Businesses in today's society have to compete in the free-enterprise system, so obviously they need qualified people to employ. Business leaders should become community exemplars in supporting every type of education system, particularly public schools. The basic challenge is for everyone not just to be a better person but also to make each life worth something, to live with vitality and care about the world, starting with the local community so that our lives can make a difference and create a better opportunity for your children and grandchildren.

Chapter Four

Health: Ensuring Our Common Wellness

Despite the drama of a year-long debate in the United States over health-care reform, no one should take great satisfaction in the modest legislative achievement in the spring of 2010. Yet compared with the last several decades of effort to create an effective, efficient, and equitable system of health care for all Americans, at least the nation has made commendable if modest progress toward a world-class public policy achievement. I say "modest," because President Obama and Congress practiced the political art of compromise to the extent that they failed to bring about the complete re-engineering that our system required — and I mean significant movement toward a universal, single-payer system. This conclusion rests on my decades of experience as a businessman and participant in community action agencies.

After my selection in 1987 as chairman of the Virginia State Board of Health, my wife Shirley and I traveled around the world and studied health care costs and related issues in Japan, Canada, England, Holland, France, Germany, Italy and the Scandinavian countries. There is one thing in common with all of those plans: Each nation provides a single-payer, government-administered payment system. The United States has yet to come to grips with the fundamental understanding that the extreme costs and relatively inferior health outcomes of using a market model for health care is not in the nation's interest, in terms of our people's physical and mental health or our country's economic well-being.

I am a Medicare recipient. Throughout my life, I have been fortunate to have health insurance coverage. As an employer, I saw to it that all of our company employees received private health care, as well as a pension plan. Our company was one of the first in Virginia's Roanoke Valley to do that, giving our employees not only economic security for their families but also ensuring a dedicated, productive work force. As a businessman, I also have always recognized the cost of health care and so am able to sympathize with the automobile industry. The burden of private coverage for autoworkers has been one of the major reasons that industry has not been able to compete globally. In addition, millions of American workers now face the prospect of losing the employer-provided coverage that for generations has been taken for granted.

Extraordinary experiences in my business and civic life have provided an awareness of the critical role that health care plays in a large, complex, diverse society like the United States. As I've related, my experience in community action agencies raised my awareness of the critical need to incorporate a health care component in virtually all the undertakings aimed at broadly opening opportunity to all. In my service with the National Academy of Sciences, I had access not only to ground-breaking studies but also to the researchers who produced them, advocating years ago such vitally important advances as adopting preventive health strategies and instituting a system of universal health care. Many people's hopes and dreams got stalled in the political traffic jam, and I came to realize then how crucial a mass movement is to motivating and sustaining broad public support for doing the right thing.

I will not mince words: The United States should have adopted a universal, single-payer health-care system long ago, just like every other modern, industrialized country. We can develop our own system, based on the experiences of Canada, England, Germany, France, the Scandinavian countries and Holland. There is no other way to adequately cover the 47 million Americans with no health insurance and a larger number with inadequate coverage.

I recall that in my experience in community organizations of all types, there has always been unanimous agreement between Democrats and Republicans about the importance of children, in education, in health care and in preparing our children for the future. Therefore, while the politicians debate the best way to get universal health insurance under a single-payer system, we should adopt immediately a comprehensive, single-payer system for all children up to the age of 6, and hopefully in time to expand that to age 18 or even 22. Health care is an absolutely essential, but of course not sufficient, condition to bring all the children, especially the poor children, into the mainstream of society and prepare them for their 13 — or preferably 17 — years of public education.

That legislation should become law as soon as possible. I still think the president should appoint a non-partisan, blue-ribbon commission of experts in health care and public finance, with the mandate to present within the following 12 months a blueprint for a new concept in financing the U.S. health-care system through a universal, single-payer structure. People with proven expertise, records of significant public and private sector service and citizens without clear vested financial interests in the health care status quo should constitute the commission. They should examine the benefits of the Department of Veterans Affairs services and the existing federal insurance options for all U.S. government employees, together with the Medicare and Medicaid programs. The commission should then compare this range of programs with each of the other advanced industrialized countries to objectively put together the best plan for the United States.

We have the specific examples from our Medicaid program and our local comprehensive Child Health Investment Program (CHIP) in Virginia's Roanoke Valley that proved without a doubt the cost-effectiveness of investing in children. Children's health care focuses primarily on prevention. Each baby covered by CHIP has a pediatrician as well as an obstetrician to deliver care, including immunization. CHIP has now expanded to include pre-natal care. Children then can enter public kindergarten in a healthy condition so that they can begin the serious learning process that we all hope continues throughout their lives. To make that possible, Congress should immediately expand Medicaid, including pre-natal care to all children up to the age of

6, with the federal government paying all the cost and relieving the states of their current requirement to match federal funds. The federal government is much better able to raise revenue than the states are with their strained budgets. Health care is an investment and not merely a sunk cost, so it would reduce health care expenditures enormously over the future generations if we immediately covered all children receiving Medicaid benefits but with the additional services that the CHIP program offers.

The value of this policy perspective became increasingly clear about the time I became chairman of the State Board of Health in 1987, an appointment that became quite newsworthy because I had been selected precisely because of my business experience. Almost immediately, I began a series of conversations with Phyllis Olin, a psychologist who worked with Head Start and also happened to be the wife of our local Congressman Jim Olin. Our first discussion came during a visit to Washington, when Shirley and I stayed with the Olins in their apartment. With my appointment as the chairman of the Board of Health, Phyllis all but challenged me to help develop a comprehensive children's health plan for Virginia. She said she would be glad to help, too. I accepted the challenge.

Some weeks later, at the invitation of Dr. Robert Blizzard, head of the University of Virginia Medical Center, I joined our family pediatrician from Salem, Dr. Doug Pierce, to meet in Charlottesville with several members of the Virginia Chapter of the American Academy of Pediatrics. The doctors sought help in creating a structure that would enhance public awareness of the need to improve children's health throughout the state. On the way home from Charlottesville, Doug Pierce and I decided that TAP should be involved and become the catalyst for organizing just such a structure, because Head Start had been successful and would make a good model from which to build a comprehensive health care program.

After a few preliminary planning sessions, TAP representatives made a list of about 30 people from all segments of the health care community in Virginia and invited them to a meeting on May 6, 1987, to discuss a comprehensive health care program for the children in the state. We brainstormed for six hours, filling up the room with white paper. When we left, we had the concept for what we named the

Comprehensive Health Investment Project, called CHIP. Its mission was to provide complete health care to children from birth to 6 years, and ensure that they grow in a healthy environment. This of course would originally be limited to low-income children, which was TAP's mission.

CHIP eventually developed into a true public/private partnership, incorporating private physicians, dentists, the local health department and TAP. The model program had three components: care coordination services, primary health care services and, as with Head Start, family support services. The program continues to operate in the same way even today. The care-coordinating service pairs a case-management nurse with the CHIP parents, who devise a long-term plan for the child's care — what's needed, who will provide it and when. The nurse acts as a link between the family and the doctor, making sure that appointments are kept, explaining follow-up care to the parent and monitoring any health problems. If needed, CHIP provides transportation. The nurse also looks for early symptoms of health problems and also monitors with each family potential situations that could impede effective care for each child.

One critical aspect of the program was providing a physician for each child. At that time, no doctor in the Roanoke area would accept Medicaid patients, including Doug Pierce and the other doctors in his practice. Once persuaded that the TAP staff monitoring would assure that patients kept their appointments, Pierce convinced physicians in his own office to accept Medicaid patients who were part of the CHIP program. He then went around to the other doctors with me and convinced all of them to accept CHIP patients. As a result, today the enrolled children immediately have a pediatrician at birth who follows them through their complete CHIP program, ideally until they go into Head Start at age 3 or 4.

TAP helped organize a separate board of directors so that CHIP could stand on its own as a non-profit and be eligible for funding. TAP applied for and received a grant of $118,000 from the Division of Maternal and Child Health of the Virginia State Health Department. That financial infusion allowed the agency to hire a nurse coordinator and two part-time health nurses and a clerk to get the program started. About 100 children were enrolled by June of 1988. All of them became patients of Doug Pierce's practice, which was called Physicians to Children. After about a year, we had 300 children because we had received another grant of $157,000 from the state.

About this same time, in my role as a member of the President's Circle of the National Academy of Sciences, we attended a forum in Washington with national speakers on the subject of child health. I met a senior official from the Kellogg Foundation, who indicated that child health was extremely critical and that Kellogg was interested in devoting significant resources to that issue. After returning to Salem, I wrote a letter to the head of the Kellogg Foundation and explained what TAP was doing through CHIP. I asked for the foundation's help. Two or three months later, I received a call, and they sent one of their staff people, Dr. Robert Hodge, who happened to be from Charlottesville originally and the University of Virginia, to Roanoke to look at the CHIP program and evaluate whether Kellogg wanted to be involved. Shortly after the meeting, Kellogg awarded TAP a four-year, $1.5 million grant specifically for CHIP's family support services, allowing an increase in staff from four people to 14 in an office of their own.

In 1990, we had 900 children assigned to the program. Kellogg was carefully monitoring our progress and was so impressed that their officials asked us to host a national conference in Roanoke for their other grantees, including Indian reservations, to study the CHIP program. The conference was very successful, so I took advantage of that opportunity to get the senior Kellogg officials together with Robert Hodge, Ted Edlich, who then was the head of the Virginia Community Action Agencies, and me as chairman of the State Board of Health. I suggested that we expand the program statewide. Kellogg responded favorably again and awarded a grant of an additional $2.3 million to set up the program in six other cities. We have subsequently received money from the U.S. Health and Human Services and a variety of other funding sources. The program has grown and is now CHIP of Virginia, a line item in the state budget. Since 1997, the federal Centers for Medicare and Medicaid Services has administered matching federal funds to states participating in the State Child Health Insurance Program, or S-CHIP. Congress did what it should have done, I like to think because of the publicity we have received on this program and the fact that Congressman Jim Olin played such a significant role to expand CHIP's reach nationwide.

The point of this story is that if I had not been involved with the Council of Community Services and had not started TAP, I never would have been appointed to the State Board of Health. That started TAP, which started CHIP, which started the expansion of CHIP, and one thing led to another until it's essentially a national program. The bottom line today is that we know even more clearly that the first six years of life are the critical part of the development of any child, and that health care is a necessary condition for the child's development and potential achievements.

Ultimately, single-payer, universal health care is a resource-allocation issue. It's cost-effective to focus on preventive health care. It's cost-effective to have health care when you need it. It's cost-effective to use prescription drugs if they work effectively to delay the onset of diseases later. I've learned in most of the health care programs we've started in an array of community action agencies that they are cost-effective. This is a basic business principle: Does it pay for itself? It would be extraordinarily cost-effective to have single-payer, universal health care. How do you pay for it? You make a national investment in it. We made a huge investment in the war in Iraq, and consider how we paid for that: We increased our national debt. But with health care, it's an investment with a progressive return on that investment over time, because within a few years costs would begin to come down everywhere, in our personal lives as well as in the federal budget. People ultimately would have more money to spend. Our businesses would be more competitive. Our people would be healthier. We'd have a huge impact on the poverty problem.

Even as Congress enacted the health-reform law in March 2010, government was already paying more than one-half of the health care costs through Medicare, Medicaid and the Department of Veterans Affairs, so the question is not whether government pays for it. The question, rather, is how much the government pays and how best to structure the system to achieve universal coverage the quickest possible way, achieving the maximum health benefits to all of our people with the least possible cost. Without question, the extreme influence gained through the decades by those with special interests in retaining the current wasteful, inadequate health-care system have fought vigorously to resist any action that curtails their enormous profits, most especially the insurance and pharmaceutical industries. Their lobbies in Washington are among the most powerful, and they have fought tooth and nail to protect their financial advantages. But those who care about the long-term health of the country, available and affordable as a matter of the public interest, must recognize that only a mass movement of civic involvement will provide such reforms. This does not mean that there is not an essential role for private health care companies just as I have with my Medicare supplemental private insurance policy. When the blue-ribbon commission, which I recommend, studies other countries such as Holland and Germany they will learn that they have developed a role for private insurance companies, but still guaranteeing universal coverage for all. The battle to improve our system goes on.

A critical aspect of revising the current system is to take business out of the payment for the delivery of health care services, which now primarily involves health insurance as an employment benefit. Such benefits, while at one time apparently serving workers' interests, create an enormous fixed cost on U.S. firms that does not fall on the competing businesses of other countries in the global marketplace. Of course, both private and public hospitals would still need to realize a profit, as would doctors' offices and clinics that provide specialty practices and therapies. Yes, even the pharmaceutical industry needs to make a profit, though not the huge one set up under the existing politically favored oligopoly that imposes unjustifiable burdens on the system. Delivery of health care, in other words, will and should continue to be delivered as much as possible through effective market mechanisms, but the payment itself should be single-payer from the federal government, exactly the same way that Social Security and Medicare are, though according to strict, comprehensive performance measures for effective medical outcomes.

In all these discussions, we must get away from the mischaracterization of "socialized medicine." Medical services themselves will be delivered by private doctors and private or non-profit hospitals and medical clinics in the private sector. It's only the payment system that would be government-run and government-paid. A part of this solution is to get away immediately from all such ridiculous ideas as health savings accounts that are tax-exempt, as President Bush recommended. That's another tax break for the wealthy and doesn't begin to solve the problems already outlined. We also need to get away from the argument that health care costs are too high because people don't pay their own medical bills and they consume too much routine care. Consumption of routine care is a small expense and can't be a major source of health care inefficiency. Look at the long lines of people standing up all night to get dental care in special clinics by well-meaning organizations and doctors that are trying to do what they can to solve the mess we're in. Remember that the bulk of all medical expenses are accounted for by a small number of people requiring expensive treatments. Remember also that we spend at least twice as much on health care as France and Britain and other industrialized countries. Some people would argue that we have better care, but statistics on longevity, infant mortality, and other medical categories do not bear out these claims. In fact, a recent study conducted by the Urban Institute reported that per-capita spending for an adult Medicare beneficiary would rise from $9,600 to $14,000 if the person were insured privately.

As a former board member of the National Foundation of Alternative Medicine, I have also become aware of emerging technologies and exploratory therapies that have not yet caught the public's attention. These nascent therapies offer promise of new avenues that the modern health-care system will need to explore, both for efficacy as well as economic efficiency. Thanks to the guidance of such leaders as Berkley Bedell, founder of the National Foundation of Alternative Medicine, new possibilities for healing remain a telling, hopeful possibility.

Despite praise from many advocates of a single-payer system in the United States, some degree of dissatisfaction exists in both the Canadian and British plans because there's a form of rationing and waiting lines. We have this in the United States as well, so there will be problems with any system. Having a single-payer plan will not solve all the health-care problems in this country. But it will solve the immediate problem of the tens-of-millions of Americans who have no health insurance and the many more Americans who have inadequate health insurance. The Urban Institute study reported that those who are uninsured often postpone needed medical care because they would be required to pay the entire cost. Some 40 percent of the uninsured have no source of regular, preventive care, which can identify and treat problems before they become acute, perhaps life-threatening. As a consequence, according to Nobel Prize-winning Princeton economist and *New York Times* columnist Paul Krugman, "the uninsured receive a lot less care than the insured. And sometimes this lack of care kills them. According to a recent estimate by the Urban Institute, the lack of health insurance leads to 27,000 preventable deaths in America each year."

In my view, the free-market ideology is wholly inappropriate in health care financing. It only increases the fragmentation of the system and the ranks of the uninsured, as the country has witnessed in the last several years. There's a huge fiscal crisis in health care. Some estimates show that even today, some people pay more for health care than they do for food. Even with the ranks of the uninsured, America still spends a much larger percentage of its gross domestic product on health care than any other industrialized country, yet we have the millions of uninsured and underinsured citizens.

One of the key inefficiencies in our health-care system has been the continued allowing of a plethora of insurance companies to act as payers for medical services. Most obvious of those inefficiencies is the 30 percent of the total cost of the U.S. health-care system swallowed up by private insurance companies. That is an unacceptable waste, especially with so much of those expenditures going to executive salaries and benefits, marketing, public relations and lobbying, not health care services. By comparison, Medicare and Medicaid provide their services with administrative costs of no more than 2 percent or 3 percent of their respective budgets. Yet another shortcoming of insurance companies has been their careful screening of policy applicants to identify and "weed out" those with a pre-existing condition who thus present a higher health risk and those who might need more-expensive treatment. The firms either rejected such applications or charged prohibitively high premiums. This not only is unfair and resulted in the terrible distortions in coverage that we have today, but it even tends to drive some of the wealthiest Americans into different insurance programs or even away from the system altogether. The American people should not tolerate the prevailing corporate indifference that in effect tells the weak, ill and aging that they're on their own. We all should insist that our political leaders begin treating health care as a service, not as a business model. The public should, in other words, demand a system that is devoted strictly to serving the nation's health by eliminating the middleman.

As pointed out in the spring of 2008 on the Public Broadcasting System program "Bill Moyers' Journal," all federal employees receive coverage under a comprehensive government program. Reporter Rick Kerr reported, "It's all government employees — members of Congress, workers at the Justice Department, and Interior, and the EPA — a total of more than 2 million people on the federal payroll. They get to choose from a wide selection of health plans — and you, the taxpayers, pay about 70 percent of their monthly premiums. Everyone within a plan — no matter how sick they are — is charged the same rate. There's no waiting period before coverage kicks in. And perhaps most importantly, no one can be denied coverage because of a pre-existing medical condition."

Such a plan now is far beyond the reach of many Americans, but it should not be. So I propose a mass movement to begin conceiving what that "ideal" universal health-care system would involve and, realistically, what may be required to phase it in over a period of time, preferably as brief as possible. In my judgment, that "ideal" would begin immediately with universal, single-payer coverage for all children up to the age of 6, as described earlier in this chapter. For other Americans not yet covered by a federally insured health system, political reality most likely would require some form of gradual phase-in over a period of years. A sweeping shift to the single-payer, universal system that Congress should adopt, but most likely will not, remains improbable in the absence of overwhelming public demand. Yet the debate must move forward, with forthright intensity, purpose and integrity in Congress, which ultimately must be held accountable by the American people for advancing the reforms that are so essential.

Whatever plan a blue-ribbon presidential commission may recommend, the fact remains that Americans who now receive their health insurance from an employer are losing that coverage rapidly. In addition, according to a 2007 study by the Kaiser Family Foundation, premiums for family coverage increased 78 percent since 2001, although wages rose by only 19 percent and inflation increased by

17 percent. Those who believe that private insurance is not a further cost on taxpayers should note that the federal government subsidizes employer-paid health insurance by exempting employer contributions from taxation as income. The value of the tax subsidy is an estimated $150 billion a year, according to Julius Richmond and Rashi Fein in their book *The Health Care Mess*. From the available and growing evidence, America's current system of providing health coverage meets the definition in classic economic theory of "market failure." Clearly, members of Congress have provided quite nicely for themselves. Providing immediate coverage for more than 300 million Americans under such a generous program would more than likely cause any member of Congress to pause, as it should in the near term. But that should not keep the commission I have proposed from taking a long, hard look at viable means of getting to that goal in as short a time as possible. That would include fully incorporating in Medicare comprehensive prescription drug coverage and gradually decreasing the age when people would qualify for Medicare. At the other end of the age spectrum, the plan could gradually increase the age ultimately to 18 for the universal coverage for children. Within a certain number of years, say 10, the two groups eventually would converge and cover the entire population in the single-payer universal system. Such an approach also would allow a decade for the insurance industry to redevelop and phase in other lines of business.

During the transition, the existing government programs could coordinate the evolution of technology developed and now operating in the Department of Veterans Affairs to compile and maintain electronic health records. Veterans Affairs also has instituted a virtual state-of-the-art system to purchase prescription drugs in huge volumes that save taxpayers millions of dollars — a practice that, thanks to the influence on Capitol Hill of the pharmaceutical industry, federal law prohibits for Medicare, thus depriving the system of a chance to achieve similar economies of scale for Medicare recipients.

Many associations and organizations across the nation are raising vocal demands to provide a single-payer universal health-care system for Americans. The Bill Moyers program on PBS revealed a case in point, the California Nurses Association. "Journal" reporter Rick Karr quoted the association's executive director, Rose Ann Demoro, as advocating universal coverage to replace the existing system: "Every registered nurse in this country advocates for her patient at the bedside. She's there. She's the last line of defense for the patients. She fights for the patients against hospital corporations, often putting her own job in jeopardy. And you can't fight for your patient without changing the social structure in which that care is delivered. So, registered nurses, organized by us, have become a pretty dramatic force in this country to change the healthcare system."

I urge others to share the realization that half-measures are no longer a worthy response to the growing crisis in U.S. health care delivery. I believe it's time for another movement. The benefits — to our children, to their graduating with excellent educations, to reducing poverty, to increasing jobs, to increasing the competitiveness of U.S. industry in globalization, to improving our environment — are such a critical issue in our society that we should organize that mass movement, beginning with each individual voter at the local level. Talk to our civic and political leaders, get together as groups and insist that our political representatives implement as quickly as possible a single-payer, universal health-care system.

Chapter Five

Environment: Sustaining Our Planet's Vitality

I am embarrassed to admit at this stage of my life that I devoted almost no genuine concern to environmental issues until about 1970. Like many other people, I just took the world almost for granted, assuming it had enough energy, clean air, reasonable population levels, fresh water and arable land to support adequately all of Mother Earth's inhabitants.

Anyone who has been paying attention in the last decade understands how shortsighted that attitude was, especially in view of the catastrophic 2010 oil spill in the Gulf of Mexico. Now, after all the education about the problems of the environment, people should insist that our political representatives do what's right and use our marketing power to force businesses to conduct themselves as good, responsible citizens. Had the American people heeded the warnings of climate change, they would have demanded three decades ago that Detroit manufacture truly energy-efficient vehicles. They would have insisted that the electric power industry — coal-fired plants being the greatest contributor in the United States to greenhouse gas emissions — generate truly clean energy. They would have demanded that all levels of government adopt sound, long-term water conservation policies. Had the public, especially business leaders and elected officials, acted on the emerging scientific evidence then, the global environment would not be under the serious strains that threaten our collective future.

In 1970, which is also the year that we took the Stuart McGuire Co. public, I was at a conference at the Massachusetts Institute of Technology and heard Professor Jay Forrester talk about his work in developing a computer model that brought together for the first time the interrelationships between population, air, water, energy, land and other factors. I had the opportunity to meet Dennis Meadows and his wife, Dana, who collaborated in writing a book called *The Limits to Growth*, based on Forrester's admittedly crude but pioneering computer model.

The Limits to Growth did not enjoy a happy reception. Many reviews called it "garbage in, garbage out." This was when the computer was in its infancy. But the book inspired many different organizations and diverse global efforts to examine environmental issues. Global models, trying to predict what would happen to the world in future generations, sprang up in eight or 10 different countries. At a 1981 conference in Austria, American University Professor John Richardson made a presentation based on his book entitled *Groping in the Dark*, which tried to compare the common ingredients of these global models. Jay Forrester and Dennis Meadows were at that conference, and I was surprised that I was the only American businessman there.

Soon after President Carter took office in 1977, he commissioned his Council on Environmental Quality to examine and reconcile U.S. environmental policies. The council director, Gus Speth, discovered that the U.S. Agency for International Development was conducting certain programs in other countries that directly conflicted with U.S. Agriculture Department policies. That evaluation and its resulting report appeared in 1980, just as President Carter was about to leave office. *The Global 2000 Report* examined what the world would look like 20 years later and beyond.

These events generally coincided with the arrival in 1974 and 1976 of new members to Congress who were amenable to studying the emerging environmental topics. The Congressional Clearinghouse of the Future organized studies and invited speakers to its monthly meetings to help create a framework for future legislation. As one of the outsiders invited to almost all of the meetings in 1977, I met then-U.S. Rep. Al Gore, who was already at the forefront of assessing the relationship of carbon dioxide (CO_2) emissions and, separately, the other greenhouse gases and their relationship to the deterioration of the Earth's ozone layer. As a founding member of the Presidents Circle of the National Academy of Sciences, I had told Gore what we had been doing and urged Congress to offer legislative support for the academy's research. I was so impressed with Gore's work that I helped to arrange for him to appear in a special program to discuss CO_2 emissions on the public television station in Roanoke.

Before that first private meeting with Gore, I already had attended two meetings of the Congressional Clearinghouse of the Future at the request of my friend, Berkley Bedell, who also was a member of Congress representing a district in Iowa. Gore was interested that I, as a businessman, could see the serious environmental problems he had been studying and asked me to come by his office. He showed me a chart that he had developed with his staff on CO_2 emissions in the air. It was dramatic. The chart is similar to the elaborate one that he exhibited in his award-winning documentary, *An Inconvenient Truth*. It's the same story. The CO_2 levels in the atmosphere have increased dramatically in the last 50 years and at an accelerating rate, which continues.

This is not to say that the CO_2 increase is the only environmental problem, but it's clear that it is a major one. What is clear, except to those with other than universal, scientific objectives to mitigate climate change, is the growing and virtually conclusive evidence of human causes for rising temperatures and greenhouse gas concentrations. Satellites since 1978 have gathered precise measurements showing no increase in the level of the sun's energy output. Rising temperatures, then, cannot be attributed to increased solar energy but to other than natural activities. According to a recent report from the National Academies, "there are no known natural factors that could explain the warming during this time period."

We know the oceans are rising, and we know the ocean temperature is warmer. We know that the glaciers worldwide are melting faster than previously measured. We know that we're over-fishing the oceans. As I mentioned above, I was basically uninformed about environmental issues until nearly a decade after Rachel Carson's 1962 book, *Silent Spring*, which began to tell the world about the problems that were developing. Since my purpose is to encourage the reader to get involved in local activities on each of the subjects presented, I hope it will be helpful for me to review what I have learned in the last three decades and the organizations that helped me with my own education and local action.

Obviously, climate change has many dimensions, but one critical aspect of environmental concerns for me has been securing sufficient fresh, clean water. As noted in an earlier chapter, I became involved in the early 1970s with helping to provide a poor rural community near my hometown with running water and sewer systems. We began the Demonstration Water Project under a Ford Foundation grant. This program is still in existence and has expanded to every state in the nation.

Yet assuring sufficient fresh water has become a looming problem that could have long-term, potentially devastating consequences unless people awaken to the potential shortages and begin to address the problems locally. We have the same amount of water that we had 50,000 years ago, no more and no less. But the oceans are rising, which means more salt water, less ground water, less fresh water. Few people realize that only 9,000 years ago, a land bridge connected what is now the British Isles and the European continent. Scientists now estimate that within 75 years, ocean levels will rise about one meter — sufficient to submerge Bangladesh and other coastal regions. Imagine Manhattan under water.

Conflicts related to fresh water are arising in the United States over the distribution of the Colorado River in the western part of the country. Tensions also are rising between Tennessee, Georgia and Florida over diverting of rivers in that region. Worldwide, because of river and stream pollution, rising sea levels caused by climate change and other preventable causes, 1 billion people lack sufficient fresh water every day. That number is growing and poses an emerging crisis that will require action locally if we are to achieve global results on the scale necessary. It's not as if we cannot see it coming. Shirley and I traveled to Alaska more than 10 years ago and saw small islands that even then were being evacuated because of rising sea levels.

One thing that we can do locally is conserve and reuse the rainwater. I am a volunteer adviser to a local company in Salem, called Rainwater Management Solutions, which has developed sophisticated procedures for capturing the rainwater from the roofs of all buildings, filtering it, and using it productively. This not only saves and reuses the water, but it also reduces the storm drain runoff, which is an additional cause of soil erosion. We can take such actions today and also insist that all new buildings and all remodeling at least save the rainwater, as we have done at our home.

In my conversation with Gore on Capitol Hill in 1977, I reminded him of my experience at MIT with Jay Forrester and Dennis and Dana Meadows, co-authors of *The Limits to Growth*. Of course, Gore had read it, but we discussed in some detail the significance of that book and Professor Forrester's first rather crude computer model. *The Limits to Growth* deals with the totality of life on the planet, and the book's title said it all.

Earlier, I had become a member of the Young Presidents Organization and later its successor, the World Business Council and the Chief Executives Organization. We traveled as small business groups to many places of the world to see what was happening in other countries and how we could apply this primarily to our own businesses and to helping our country. One meeting was conducted at the Houston Space Center, and a major presentation showed photographs from space that had been taken over a 10-year period clearly showing how the climate was changing in different parts of the globe. We focused on Western Canada, where the photos revealed that in that decade the climate was changing. Some climate scientists were predicting at that conference that if this continued for another 50 years, the growing season in Western Canada would be so short that the farmers would not be able to grow wheat, the staple crop for the region.

What has become obvious — and has been progressively obvious for many years now — is that we are overusing our resources and are putting at least twice as much CO_2 into the atmosphere as it can absorb. *Earth: The Sequel*, by Fred Krupp, is one of the best books on the problems of climate change. I served more than three years with Krupp, now president of the Environmental Defense Fund, at the Heinz Center for Science, Economics, and the Environment. As he noted in his book, passage of the Clean Air Act in 1990 radically altered the environmental paradigm by soliciting the cooperation of U.S. industries to reduce acid rain through the cap-and-trade system of sulfur dioxide emission controls. That same approach, Krupp argues, would substantially improve the current problem of carbon emissions. "Worldwide, nations must cut emissions in half over the next 50 years," Krupp writes, "and to reach that goal the United States will have to cut emissions by 80 percent."

To achieve that objective, he correctly argues, policy should create financial incentives and business opportunities that will attract the nation's entrepreneurs eager to get involved and unleash the American creative genius to develop the technology that will reduce the climate change threats. Krupp closes his book with the observation: "We have before us an extraordinary opportunity: to harness the power of the United States of America's huge and dynamic markets to ensure a safe future. None of us any longer can stand by and watch; all of us must engage as citizens to demand that our country lead the world to solve the climate crisis."

I would add to that: All we need is for everyone to take action, beginning at the local level, first understanding the problem and then being determined to do something individually and collectively to help.

Dr. John Sterman, the Jay W. Forrester Professor of Management at MIT said in a recent lecture, "The science is unequivocal now, and the scientists are telling us that it's urgent that we reduce emissions. The debate is basically done, but the public at large still does not understand that." Sterman said that the greenhouse gas-induced climate change is not enough to stabilize carbon dioxide at the current level or to curb the levels slightly, but he indicated how critical it is to start to reduce the carbon dioxide concentrations in the atmosphere. He used a simple example of an overflowing bathtub: Even if the drain on the tub is open when the inflow of water exceeds the outflow, the water level will rise over time, and eventually the tub will overflow.

James Gustave "Gus" Speth, President Carter's chairman of the Council on Environmental Quality and the former dean of the School of Forestry and Environmental Studies and the Sara Shallenberger Brown Professor in the Practice of Environmental Policy at Yale and my long-time friend, recently said it another way in his new book, *The Bridge at the Edge of the World*: "How serious are the threats to our environment? Here is one measure of the problem. If we continue to do exactly what we're doing, with no growth in the human population or the world economy, the world in the latter part of this century will be unfit to live in. Of course, human activities are not holding at current levels — they are accelerating dramatically, and so, too, is the pace of climate disruption, biotic impoverishment and toxification."

Speth contends that this critique leads to a "severe indictment of today's economic and political system — capitalism as it now actually operates. Our vital task is to change the operating instructions for the modern economy before it's too late."

I first met Speth during the Carter administration. He recommended to President Carter that the administration conduct a major analysis of the goals and activities of each federal agency so the government could adopt a coordinated policy and prevent having one department operate in conflict with another. As mentioned before, this led to the publication in 1980 of *The Global 2000 Report*, which was another effort to predict what would happen to this country and the world if present trends continued. After President Carter left office and started the Carter Center in Atlanta, Speth taught for a while and then organized the World Resources Institute, which I helped modestly and have stayed in touch with since. This is now a premier research organization in Washington, led by its president, Jonathan Lash. Speth became head of the United Nations Development Program for 10 years, working to alleviate both poverty and environmental deterioration on a global basis.

George Mitchell is a Houston energy executive, developer and generous advocate for education and the environment. I met Mitchell in the Young President's Organization and have remained friends with him for decades. As one of the early supporters of Dennis Meadows at MIT, he had purchased hundreds of copies of *The Global 2000 Report* and mailed one to each of the Fortune 500 chief executive officers in the United States to call their attention to these global issues. He started the Houston Area Research Center and the Woodlands Conference, in which he asked me to participate. Since that time, he's had periodic conferences and given The Mitchell Prize, a $100,000 award at each conference, to encourage research into environmental and growth issues. There is indeed a limit to growth. Mitchell, who has spent more time and personal resources than anyone I know in supporting research and public awareness of environmental concerns, said some years ago, "The world is not working with 6 billion people. How can it work with 50 percent more?"

As a result of these and other close business, civic and personal relationships, I was fortunate to become involved with the National Academy of Sciences, including a role in the formation of the President's Circle at the academy. I had the good fortune also to meet Frank Press, the scientific adviser to President Carter and later president of the National Academy of Sciences for 12 years.

One particularly dramatic example of the effectiveness of that web of relationships developing in the small but growing group of environmental advocates was a private meeting I had helped to arrange in 1981 that included Al Gore, Frank Press, Elkin Blount of Harvard and myself. We urged Gore to take a lead in Congress in helping the Academy of Sciences do basic research into climate change, CO_2 emissions and other environmental problems. During that meeting, Gore asked me whether I was familiar with the Gaia Theory. I replied that I was generally aware of it, but he explained further that it was an ecological hypothesis proposing that living and nonliving parts of the earth are a complex interacting system that can be thought of as a single organism. The theory postulates that all living things have a regulatory effect on the Earth's environment that promotes life overall. When he finished explaining, he took a piece of yellow paper and drew a graphic representation of the theory. We knew then we had a worthy congressional advocate. I still have that graph in my file. A small picture of it is in the back of this book.

Not long after that session, Speth led Press, Mitchell and me to Atlanta where President Carter had established his Carter Center. We had hoped to draw the Center into an active role to produce programs that improve understanding and awareness of environmental issues, which the center has continued to do. Since that time, the National Academy of Sciences also has set up special environmental departments. With Mitchell's generous contribution of $10 million, an entire sustainable development center has come into being with its own Web page, publishing many articles and a very important book, *Our Common Journey*, which emphasizes that the problems we're talking about are global and not just limited to the United States.

I became fascinated with these important and exciting trends and decided to try to do something in my own local community in Southwest Virginia. After I sold my business in 1986 and started the Cabell Brand Center at Roanoke College, the center was successful in developing a regional partnership among colleges in the area, and we put together a group to sponsor a sustainable development conference at Hollins College in 1987. The conference brought together representatives from business, federal and state governments, non-government organizations and the academic community. That three-day conference with a variety of workshops led to the formation of local committees to continue to study and develop local programs to help educate the local population about environmental awareness and to mitigate the continuing problems. A couple of years later, Roanoke College asked our center to put together a hunger conference, at which Gus Speth was the keynote speaker. We agreed to do that as long as we didn't limit it to hunger. We talked about the cause of hunger, which again was a symptom of people not participating in society, of being impoverished, marginalized and left with inadequate resources to purchase or grow their food.

That event was followed a couple of years later at nearby Ferrum College with another major conference on sustainable development. The keynote speaker was Ray Anderson, president of Interstate Carpet, a leading firm in developing strategies to run a Fortune 500 business with almost zero negative effects on the environment and minimum energy consumption. He subsequently won a Mitchell Prize at the Woodlands Conference.

In each of those conferences at Hollins, Roanoke College and Ferrum, as well as the annual Environment Virginia Conference at Virginia Military Institute, we urged participants to sign up as a volunteer for some local action group. We encouraged the local groups to participate with the national environmental organizations, such as the Sierra Club, to increase local participation in activities. This compelling goal of becoming involved locally is something we all need to accelerate, following the commendable example of VMI's annual conferences, held now for 30 years. Governors have appeared along with representatives of corporations, non-government organizations and each department of the state government to hear and discuss the problems of Virginia in these changing times. Former Governor Tim Kaine was truly assertive with his administration's climate change commission, which set a splendid example of what Virginia must do in the next generation, particularly with its large coastal area threatened by the inevitable rise of the oceans. Governors in other states should take note and emulate Kaine's exemplary leadership.

So, yes, we have begun to pay attention and have come some of the way necessary to make a favorable difference in preserving the essential environmental properties without which we cannot indefinitely sustain our quality of life. Thus in the last 30 years, some gains have been made in trying to advance public understanding of the environmental problems facing society, as documented by Al Gore in his *An Inconvenient Truth*, which won him an Academy Award and eventually a Nobel Peace Prize. But in spite of Gore's work, contrarian opinions and denial still persist, particularly within the federal government. As Gore pointed out in his award-winning documentary, many officials with the Environmental Protection Agency have been inclined to address climate change. Unfortunately, they were suppressed by senior political officials within the administration of George W. Bush, who censored scientific work by the agency's career employees. For the American public, the education process is far from over.

Understanding the implications of environmental deterioration has become critical, and understanding the need to act locally as well as globally is more essential than ever. My intense awareness came in 1990 when I met Rebecca Adamson of the First Nations Development Organization. She had been working to assist, first, U.S. Native Americans and then indigenous people in other parts of the world suffering from environmental deterioration that results in poverty, land rights and the lack of economic development. Much of my own awareness of such matters was aided by the ability to actually go to such places that Rebecca Adamson serves. After I sold my business in 1986, I was asked to serve for two years as a consultant with the United Nations Development Program to try to build up the shoe industry in Bangladesh. Hides and finished leather were relatively abundant there, but the country had no real manufacturing capability. My wife Shirley and I made several trips to Bangladesh to try to establish a nascent industry, eventually helping to set up one factory that unfortunately was flooded and then rebuilt. The challenges were daunting, especially in a land where the average elevation is one foot above sea level.

Then we followed the same process of advising the U.N. program for initiatives in India, Egypt and Botswana. Each country presented us with insights and painful reminders of the various environmental perils that pose the constant threat of disaster. Few experiences open a person's eyes to such calamities like actually being present in the midst of such struggle and want, but I believe that such experience can awaken in each of us the desire to help reverse needless degradation of the environment — beginning locally and extending it globally.

Having been fortunate to experience such fascinating encounters, I received yet another opportunity to draw upon those encounters with my six-year service from 1990 to 1996 on the board of The Heinz Center for Science, Economics, and the Environment, along with Tom Lovejoy, a national environmental leader who led the Smithsonian Institution environmental program for many years, The Heinz Center brought to my attention early research on the oceans and climate changes as revealed in ice core samples from the Antarctic. Knowledge has been increasing, and fortunately many organizations began to grow out of the early examples set by World Future Society, the Sierra Club and even the more radical Greenpeace. The Heinz Center has produced particularly excellent work, which includes a periodic report sponsored by the Environmental Protection Agency, cataloging the ecosystems of the United States through an attempt to chart the increasing problems throughout our country on resource depletion, river pollution, rising oceans and every other critical environmental index. There are opportunities today for each of us to participate locally in helping to mitigate the identified problems.

I don't believe the public generally realizes that oil supplies in the world are finite and are declining, with no new major oil discoveries on the horizon. There have been speeches by some politicians recommending a major national effort to create alternative energy sources, much like the Manhattan Project that developed the atomic bomb. The objective, first, would be to reduce the cost of energy; second, to help the environment; third, to stop our dependence on foreign oil; and fourth, to strengthen our economy with about half of our trade deficit going to pay for foreign oil. This issue has gotten the public's attention, and the federal government must make massive investments in alternative energy to attack this problem quickly.

With regard to the energy debate, I feel there have been some misinterpretations of Al Gore's comments and promotion of ethanol and the use of coal. The federal government made a grave mistake in granting subsidies to corn for ethanol, which has contributed to the high cost of food in today's marketplace. This doesn't mean that ethanol should not be produced, but it should be developed on a commercial scale using crop waste, wood waste, perennial grasses and other plants to produce what is called cellulosic ethanol, and not concentrate on food crops. Al Gore's book "Our Choice" clearly shows how the U.S. can become energy independent--if we have the will.

In laying out our future plans, we must recognize that in the short term, coal inevitably is going to be a major source of our energy, even as we use hybrid automobiles and rely on electricity to recharge these cars. Most of our electricity in the United States is generated today by coal, which will be used throughout the world in the next 100 years. In fact, China is putting a new coal-fired plant in operation every week, which gives that rising industrial power the energy to reduce its oil imports. As with so many other areas in the world, Chinese oil reserves are fast depleting. India also is virtually exploding in its demands for energy, marking yet another complex factor in the equation of arriving at some international consensus on reducing the human impact on climate change. The United States probably cannot afford to discontinue the use of coal abruptly, and several plants are under construction now. The role of the United States immediately should be to gather together all of the best information about the least-worst way to use coal: What kind of coal? How best to scrub it and as nearly as possible eliminate the CO_2 emissions? What is the arithmetic of gasification and liquefaction? The United States is in a position to be a leader in technology in the least-worst way to use coal and insist with our influence that these practices be adopted worldwide. We should start setting the right example and refuse to grant a grandfather clause for existing coal-fired plants. Rather, they should be refitted immediately to reduce their emissions. The technology exists. All we need is the will, and of course the resources. Hopefully, one day, coal will not be necessary, but it will be for the foreseeable future in the transition to alternative fuels.

Another controversial energy source is nuclear generation, which will be a major player, but it takes 10 years from start to finish to build a new nuclear plant. We need to learn from the French not only the most efficient way to use nuclear energy but also their new technology for recycling the spent fuel and cores left from old nuclear plants, where no safe storage place has been found. The French have developed a new reprocessing technique, even though there is some residue from it. But technology can be used to solve this problem.

With the long term uncertainty of petroleum based fuels, the market system is beginning to speak up, with plans under way for mass production of electric vehicles and use of technology to increase wind power and solar energy with more sophisticated storage capacities. Nevertheless, in the short term, conservation is the first step and is the way that each of us, in our own way, can reduce energy consumption.

As current National Academy of Sciences President Ralph J. Cicerone told the 145th annual meeting of the academy in April 2008, "We must assure access to energy and geopolitical security, overcome the financial impact of high costs, deal with climate change, other environmental impacts, nuclear safety and wastes. There is no simple single solution and some attractive options are mutually incompatible."

I am encouraged to see movements such as the Corporate Ecosystem Services Review, which helps managers of corporations develop strategies to manage business risks and opportunities in their own companies. The World Resources Institute, started by my friend Gus Speth and continued by Jonathan Lash, who spoke at the VMI Environmental Conference in 2007, collaborated with the World Business Council for Sustainable Development to establish this Ecosystems Review. Fortunately, climate change concerns are rising to the top of the corporate agenda. Such movements are in the right direction.

I remember a presentation at an Academy of Sciences meeting a few years ago by Sherry Rowland, a Nobel Prize winner who discovered the hole in the ozone over the Antarctic. Rowland predicted that because of the nitric oxide from automobile exhaust in Asia in 20 years, with the trade winds bringing that air into the United States, no U.S. city would be able to comply with current EPA clean-air standards, much less the tighter regulations scheduled for implementation in the near future. The public needs to understand fully the importance of the air we breathe, the water we drink and the energy we consume.

The National Academy of Sciences in its recent publication, "Climate Change," said, "A growing body of evidence indicates that the Earth's atmosphere is warming. Much of this increase has occurred since 1978. We observe that changes in oceans, ecosystems and the ice cover are consistent with this warming trend. The fact is that the Earth's climate is always changing. Greenhouse gases have increased significantly since the Industrial Revolution, mostly from the burning of fossil fuels for energy, industrial processes and transportation. Greenhouse gases are at their highest levels in at least 400,000 years and continue to rise."

We still don't know how much, how fast and where these effects will take place. Scientists are just beginning to project how climate science might affect regional weather. In fact, the phrase "climate change" is growing in preferred use to "global warming," because it helps convey that there are changes in addition to rising temperatures. Al Gore, in accepting the Nobel Peace Prize, said, "We, the human species, are confronting a planetary emergency, a threat to the survival of our civilization that is gathering ominous and destructive potential even as we gather here, but there's hopeful news as well. We have the ability to solve this crisis and avoid the worst, though not all, of its consequences, if we act boldly, decisively and quickly."

Yet how we act also must consider an ethical dimension. Writing in *Scientific American* magazine in June 2008, Oxford moral philosopher John Broome wrote, "What should we do about climate change? The question is an ethical one. Science, including the science of economics, can help discover the causes and effects of climate change. It can also help work out what we can do about climate change. But what we should do is an ethical question. If the world is to do something about climate change, some people — chiefly the better-off among the current generation — will have to reduce their emissions of greenhouse gases to save future generations from the possibility of a bleak existence in a hotter world. When interests conflict, 'should' questions are always ethical."

And that's our job — you, the reader, and me and our friends and associates at the local level — to ask those hard questions of ourselves, and to do everything that we can to reduce energy consumption, greenhouse gas emissions, and overuse of the Earth's resources. The American public needs to understand that on our planet, it's all finite. We have only so much land, so much air, so much water and so much of the other resources that we take from the ground. Years ago, Mahatma Gandhi said, "Earth provides enough to satisfy every man's need, but not every man's greed."

The basic issue is one of sustainable development, which was defined in 1987 by the United Nations Brundtland Commission as "meeting the needs of the present without compromising the ability of future generations to meet their own needs." Gro Brundtland has been a leader in Europe and the world for many environmental initiatives. My wife and I met her in Norway, and she became one of the seven fellows established by our Cabell Brand Center at Roanoke College.

The National Academy of Sciences also has assessed these related difficulties and has issued the following statement: "Global environmental changes such as climate change and deforestation are the result of unsustainable patterns of development. Changes in climate, in turn, may pose challenges to future development, to have impacts on critical natural resources and the health and economic well-being of people, especially those in less-developed and coastal regions of the world."

The academy's National Research Council carries out a variety of studies, workshops and meetings, and publishes numerous reports on science policy issues related to sustainability. The public is invited to participate in its very sophisticated Web site: http://sustainability.nationalacademies.org/.

At the 2008 Environmental Conference at VMI, keynote speaker Professor John Ikerd from the University of Missouri said, "The greatest ecological uncertainties confronting the United States are global in nature. At no time in human history have we faced environmental risks comparable to those of global climate change and 'peak oil.' Even the major oil companies now grudgingly admit that global production of petroleum has peaked and that the world is beginning to run out of fossil energy. Yet many Americans remain in denial. We continue to roll back environmental regulations that protect our air and water, and refuse to sign treaties to protect the global environment. In a futile attempt to squeeze a little bit more economic value from our badly depleted natural resources, Americans eventually must accept the 'Inconvenient Truth' that we are at serious risk of making Earth uninhabitable by humans."

Ikerd concluded his remarks with these words: "Yes, we live in uncertain times. The ecological, social and economic risks confronting our nation and society today are unprecedented. Never have the decisions of so few threatened the survival of humanity, and never has the responsibility of humanity rested on the shoulders of so many. A sustainable economy cannot be built or constructed. It must be conceived, nurtured and grown to maturity from the grassroots up. A consensus for a sustainable society cannot be mandated or decreed. It must be born in and must grow among individuals, families, communities and nations. Fortunately, we have everything we need to create a sustainable economy and a sustainable society. We know how to do what needs to be done. We simply need to find the courage to do it."

While taking inventory of increasing global environmental problems, we should not overlook the local action that is taking place all over the United States to achieve greater compliance with Leadership in Environmental and Engineering Design standards, or LEED certification. In Roanoke, our two new museums and even the regional jail are being built to LEED certification, which makes efficient use of energy, air, water, construction materials and every other aspect of what is currently called the "green building movement." Much of this started under the world-famous architect, William McDonough, who published in 2002 a history-making book entitled *Cradle to Cradle: Remaking the Way that We Make Things.* Formerly the dean of architecture at the University of Virginia, McDonough has been commissioned to design sustainable cities in China, where people can live and work in the same place and have buildings that meet LEED certification.

Two young Roanoke graduates of the Yale School of Architecture, Greg and Jennifer Lewis, are devoting their lives to green building. They organized a 2006 international home design competition called "C to C," or Cradle to Cradle, in which McDonough and other world-class architects judged hundreds of designs from forward-thinking students and professional architects from all over the world who were challenged to create homes that achieved new standards of sustainability. More than 600 answered the call.

Appalachian Sustainable Development is another Southwestern Virginia program that seeks to use local resources to help rather than deplete the natural resources of the area. The program also promotes businesses that sell sustainably harvested lumber and local organic food products.

I am encouraged by the number of local organizations that are emerging to promote local sustainable development in all products, particularly food and building materials. This is the type of grassroots movement we need to solve the array of environmental issues confronting the world. We just need to multiply those participating in that action by hundreds of thousands.

Acting locally may have little direct bearing on international policies, but determined advocacy at the local level by Americans — the world's contributors of the largest amount of CO_2 and nitrous oxide emissions — can also demand that their government lead the way and offer examples of model conduct and development of new energy technologies to restrain the damage being done to our common home: Earth. The challenge now is for everyone locally to pick up the chant — from each household, community, state and nation — and realize that the planet's resources are finite. Such concerns are nothing less than essential for America's long-term national security. We must accept the challenge to provide for ourselves, and those who follow us, the clean energy, clean air and clean water that a just, prosperous and peaceful society should bequeath to future generations.

Chapter Six

Racial Justice: Making Room for All

On Saturday, August 11, 2007, former Gov. Tim Kaine of Virginia called my wife Shirley and me and invited us to come the next day to the governor's house in Richmond for a private viewing with the family of Oliver Hill, who had died a few days earlier. Hill had been the last surviving member of the legal team headed by the future Supreme Court Justice Thurgood Marshall that argued the case before the U.S. Supreme Court, leading to the landmark *Brown vs. Board of Education* school desegregation decision of 1954. Gov. Kaine had remembered that my wife and I had a hand in starting the Oliver Hill Foundation, and that just two months before he died, more than 1,000 people had gathered in Richmond at a marvelous celebration of his 100th birthday. All the living governors of Virginia joined the commemoration, paying tribute and even asking forgiveness for the years of massive resistance against racial integration that resulted in the state's closing of public schools after *Brown vs. Board of Education* ruling of the Supreme Court in 1954. Fortunately, Hill was able to be there and offered some brief, gracious and eloquent remarks, summoning those gathered there that evening to continue the healing of racial divisions still lingering in our society.

Gathering at the governor's mansion with others to pay our final respects to Oliver Hill, my wife and I recalled how the last several years of acquaintance with him had inspired us to help initiate the Oliver

Hill Foundation. He had been committed to providing opportunities for black students to be interns as well as students in law schools in Virginia. Between respectful whispers among those at the viewing, I reflected on memories from those last six or seven years during which I was privileged to spend a good deal of time with him. Then my eye fixed on a small plaque engraved on Hill's casket: "May the work I have done speak for me." Those words made a deep, powerful impression on me. That was the day that I decided to write this book, because the elusive quest for racial and social justice is one of the major barriers that prevents our country from realizing its most precious ideals as proclaimed by the Declaration of Independence and the Bill of Rights to the U.S. Constitution. Oliver Hill lived his life to achieve those ideals, and the duty of citizenship summons each of us in our society to do everything we can to assure that race and ethnic origin are absolutely immaterial. Unfortunately, we are a long way from that, as is the world, with the ethnic strife in the Middle East, in Bosnia, in different countries in Africa and seemingly everywhere. But the United States of America must be the shining light of a society that creates an equal opportunity for everyone, regardless of race or ethnic origin. That's our individual, personal responsibility to reclaim the American dream.

During the 2008 presidential campaign, two Democratic candidates competed for the nomination, one black and one female, for the first time in the history of the country. It is a historic source of shame that slavery existed in the United States when the Declaration of Independence and Constitution were adopted. It took the Civil War with its tragedy and huge loss of life and physical destruction to bring about the Emancipation Proclamation by President Abraham Lincoln. That historic proclamation was only the first step toward achieving a just society in which race is irrelevant. It took nearly 100 years after the end of the Civil War before the Supreme Court in the Brown education decision ruled that racial discrimination had no place in our public schools. It took another 20 years before Congress passed the civil rights legislation that guaranteed the right to vote and finally established the legal protections for equal treatment under law.

The one question that people have asked me for the last 40 or 50 years is why I think the way I do with regard to race relations and why I do the things that I have done in the various business, civic and political endeavors in my life. I can't answer that question precisely, but one experience from my youth has been seared indelibly in my memory. When I was only 8 or 9 years old, I asked my father for a nickel to ride a new bus line that had just been put in operation in the 1930s, during the Depression. A girl living with us from the Baptist Children's Home took me on the bus, but I couldn't see out the window from the seat where we were sitting. So I got up and went to the back row, because the seats in the back of the bus were higher. The bus driver stopped the bus, went back and took me by the hand and told me to sit where I was supposed to sit because that back seat was for "n_____." I couldn't understand that, but as the bus ride continued, I went to the back seat again, thinking the driver didn't see me. Two or three times he stopped the bus and brought me back to my seat. When we got home, Beulah, the girl who was with me, told my father, who spanked me for not obeying the rules on the bus and for sitting with the "n_____." Unquestionably, that's the way my mother and father looked at the situation in the 1930s, indeed, even throughout their lives.

I had always attended all-white, segregated schools, including VMI, which did not accept blacks until 1968. My first real experience in seeing racial injustice was during World War II, when even our own military services were not integrated. But one of the moving experiences in the war for me was to see groups of starving people being liberated from the concentration camps of Hitler's Germany. I could not understand such inhumanity.

When I came back after the war and started to build the shoe business in 1949, we had door-to-door sales people who took orders that were returned in the mail. We had no idea whether the orders were from a white person or a black person. But as I visited our salesmen across the country and conducted sales meetings, I could see segregation almost at its worst before the Brown education decision. I could not take our black sales people into a white restaurant. In the early 1950s, I conducted a sales meeting in a New Orleans hotel, and about one-third of the participants were black. The security guards from that hotel came to me and said that we had to shut down the meeting and the black people had to leave, because they were not welcome as guests. I told them it was a private room, I had paid for it and that I would take them to court if they created any problem. I had no help, but actually pushed a security guard out of the door and shut it. The scene was tense, but the meeting progressed. Unfortunately, I had a number of similar experiences during those troubling years in the transition from a segregated society.

I was determined in my business to do as much as I could to build a strong team of employees, and that meant treating all of them in ways that would result in the greatest level of productivity and return on investment. In the shoe business, our factories were on piecework, and we paid people in accordance with how many uppers they stitched, or whatever task they performed. There was no distinction between black and white.

During this period, I continued to have problems within my own family. A friend of mine at the Yale Law School wrote me that he was driving from New England with his black roommate to Dallas and would like to spend the night in Roanoke. But he indicated that he was concerned about the prospects of repercussions from the South's Jim Crow laws on his friend. Of course, I invited them to stay with me, but I needed an extra blanket and a pillow. I asked my mother for them, and she replied that she did not have "n_____ cover." I've never forgotten that regrettable encounter.

Once the business began to grow, I became increasingly active in the Young Presidents Organization. I led a trip to South Africa when apartheid was in its prime in the late 1960s. I was interviewed by one of the local newspapers and asked if we were planning to open any factories in South Africa. I said, "No, not until you pay equal pay for equal work, regardless of race." On that trip, we had one of the first integrated business meetings with the mayor of Soweto , the black community in Johannesburg, but we had to do it in a private room in a hotel in Johannesburg that was willing to take the risk.

Back home, in the "land of the free," I was invited in 1960 to become a member of the Shenandoah Club in Roanoke, a private social club organized in 1893 and which allowed only white males in its membership for nearly a century. When I learned that they did not accept blacks, Jews or women, I declined the invitation.

By 1998, one of my VMI friends, Howard Lawrence, came to my office and asked me if I would help the Shenandoah club bring in a number of black members. They already had accepted one, in addition to some Jewish members and one woman. I agreed to help, and therefore joined the club, which now has adopted the principle that race is irrelevant as a criterion for membership.

Progress toward racial inclusiveness had been just as resistant in Salem a little more than a decade after that first overture from the Shenandoah Club. In 1977, I was asked by the Salem Rotary Club to become a candidate for district governor of this district for Rotary International. I told the board of directors that I would consider doing so if I were elected, but that my agenda would include trying to integrate the Rotary Clubs in this district, which at that point still did not have any black or women members. I reminded the club that at the previous district conference, the president of Rotary International had expressed satisfaction and pride that his greatest accomplishment during his year in office was to integrate the Rotary Club of Johannesburg, South Africa. I figured that if Rotary could integrate a club in South Africa, we could integrate a Virginia district of Rotary International. The club board enthusiastically and unanimously approved my condition, and I was elected district governor. At the first opportunity, I submitted for membership in the Salem Rotary Club a black friend of mine, Morris Elam, whom I had known with his family for two generations. He agreed to join the club if he were accepted, and I told him the whole story of what we were trying to do. Unfortunately, when the club voted on Elam's membership, at least two Rotary members blackballed him, which meant that his membership was rejected. That vote posed a serious problem for me as a matter of principle. I wrote an extensive letter to the club members in September of 1977 and explained my position. I told them that without the support of my local club, I certainly could not accomplish what I wanted to do as district governor, so I resigned that office after having been elected at the district conference.

I did not resign from the club immediately because I did not want to disparage the club publicly. I waited about six months before quietly resigning. About 10 years later, Salem Rotary Club began to accept black members, and after that women as well. In 2007, I received a letter from the president of Salem Rotary Club inviting me back into the club and asking me to be an honorary member without having to pay dues. In a matter of months, they honored me by presenting me the citizen of the year award of the club.

As president of the Roanoke Touchdown Club in 1962, I was pleased to help break new ground in another realm of local community life as well. The Roanoke Touchdown Club presented an annual award to the best local football player. That year, Charles "Big Dog" Thornhill was unquestionably the most qualified player in the area, but because he was black, his name did not appear on the list of nominees. I insisted that his name appear on the ballot, and fortunately, Thornhill received the award. The occasion caused some consternation at the hotel where the banquet was to be held, though, because the hotel had never served blacks. I told the manager of the hotel in advance what we were doing and invited the Thornhill family as guests. Bear Bryant, the Alabama football coach, was the speaker. Although de facto segregation in Alabama was no less prohibitive of Bryant's accepting a black recruit in the early 1960s, he was eventually instrumental in helping Thornhill receive a football scholarship from 1964-66 at Michigan State, where he was an All-Big Ten linebacker on two national championship teams. The sad aspect of that story was that a genuine local sports luminary had to leave his community to gain the opportunities that allowed him to excel.

Another of the biggest frustrations, if not disappointments, to me during the '50s and '60s was the reluctance of the churches to attempt to integrate. In fact, Martin Luther King's original idea for the Selma march had been to integrate the churches. That objective only in time developed into the vast movement leading to the nation's civil rights legislation. Even today, the most segregated part of our society is at 11 o'clock on Sunday morning in the black and white churches. Racial segregation persists within denominations. Even in 2008, President Jimmy Carter convened a major conference in Atlanta to try to bring the black and white churches together along with his Baptist followers to unite them all in racial and social solidarity.

I was encouraged by the occasional bursts of inspiration from presidential candidates during the 2008 campaign, especially the speech by Barack Obama in his reply to criticisms of his minister and even of his wife concerning matters of race. In his Philadelphia speech of March 2008, he said, "The fact is that the comments that have been made recently and the issues that have surfaced over the last few weeks reflect the complexities of race in this country that we've never really worked through, a part of our union that we have yet to perfect. And if we walk away now, if we simply retreat into our respective corners, we will never be able to come together and solve challenges like health care or education or the need to find good jobs for every American."

That speech reminded me of another sales meeting I had in Montgomery, Alabama, which happened to coincide with the day, Jan. 14, 1963, when George Wallace was inaugurated as governor of Alabama. Wallace stood at the podium and said, "Segregation now, segregation forever!" Not until federal troops would intervene in Alabama, Arkansas, Mississippi and other states did the public schools in those states become integrated, yet — as Obama's words captured with troubling precision — society today has yet to resolve completely the more subtle implications of separate and unequal.

In the more than four decades that Total Action Against Poverty has served the Roanoke Valley, I have been proud of the role that community action agency has played in the service of racial justice, especially in light of the endemic racism in Virginia in the mid-1960s when we began our initial program, Head Start. Poor white families resisted sending their children to school with blacks. Bedford County officials steadfastly refused to allow the program because it was integrated. We look back now and note that of the more than 30,000 children who have benefited from TAP's Head Start, 60 percent have been African-American. Similarly, all of TAP's programs have significantly contributed to ameliorating the effects of poverty for blacks through programs aimed at improving housing, health care and job training, including transition assistance statewide for more than 25,000 former inmates, the vast majority of whom in Virginia prisons are African-American.

After the public schools became integrated, we began to notice that few black students were going to college. TAP commissioned a study with the assistance of Norm Fintel, president of Roanoke College, to learn why. We were troubled to learn that neither teachers nor counselors were encouraging the black children in the fourth, fifth and sixth grades to prepare themselves for high school. When they arrived at high school, the students received no encouragement to take college-bound courses. They were on what we called the "black track" in public high schools, which ruled out taking the critical courses in math, science, advanced English and other challenging studies. Unfortunately, if they did go to the university, there was a high dropout rate because they did not have the academic background to succeed.

So TAP arranged a federal education grant to initiate a program, dubbed Project Discovery, intended to motivate students in sixth, seventh and eighth grades to prepare for college. They went on college tours, were offered assistance with study skills and received help with entrance-exam preparation and college applications. TAP helped to replicate more than 20 Project Discovery programs throughout the state. More than 900 students in the TAP service area were the first members of their families to attend college, with statewide figures showing 8,000 young people having achieved that goal. In those programs and counting some financial aid made available, TAP has helped more than 10,000 black youths in Virginia graduate from college simply by intervening at the middle school level to inspire and motivate the students.

For all these years and in so many diverse ways, TAP continues to prove itself a beneficial force of local advocacy to open doors and level the playing fields of opportunity, regardless of race. Yet TAP always has operated on the unassailable principle that with opportunity comes responsibility. The agency's offering "a hand up and not a handout" continues to require that clients honor their end of the bargain as well by seeking job training and employment, and abandoning destructive behaviors that lead to hopelessness, substance abuse and even crime. That applies particularly to men and women who too often have been willing to abandon their responsibilities not only to themselves but especially to their children, far too many of them born out of wedlock. Comedian and author Bill Cosby in the last few years has led a somewhat controversial personal campaign to challenge black men to face up to those responsibilities. As Cosby told writer Ta-Neshi Coates for an article published in the May 2008 edition of *The Atlantic* magazine, "What do I need if I am a child today? I need people to guide me. I need the possibility of change. I need people to stop saying I can't pull myself up by my own bootstraps."

One of the most humbling and gratifying episodes of my life was the invitation my wife and I received from black cadets at VMI in 1992 to attend a special ceremony at the campus and to receive the first Jonathan Daniels Award, presented for my contributions to advancing civil rights over the years. The Promaji Club — an organization of VMI cadets promoting positive relations among all races and ethnic groups among the Corps of Cadets and so named from the Swahili word for "fellowship" — had originally instituted the Jonathan Daniels Award, but it graciously granted the Board of Visitors exclusive use of the name to strengthen the institutional foundation of the award.

Daniels was the valedictorian for the VMI Class of 1961. After graduating, he attended the Episcopal Divinity School in Cambridge, Mass., where he was ordained as a priest, and answered the call of Martin Luther King Jr. in January of 1965 to help with his Selma to Montgomery march. Among Daniels's duties was helping black people register to vote, because the white establishment had created every possible obstacle toward letting blacks go to the polls. Condemned by local officials as an "outside agitator," Daniels used his own body to shield a young black girl, Ruby Sales, at whom a white deputy sheriff had aimed a shotgun with the intention of killing her. Daniels absorbed the blast and died instantly. The deputy was acquitted in two trials, one local and one federal, by all-white juries. When notified of the incident, Martin Luther King Jr. said: "One of the most heroic Christian deeds of which I have heard in my entire ministry was performed by Jonathan Daniels. Certainly there are no incidents more beautiful in the annals of church history, and though we are grieved at this time, our grief should give way to a sense of Christian honor and nobility."

Such is the legacy of terrible sacrifice to bring racial healing, and I am proud of the legacy that VMI has chosen to embrace. It wasn't always so. I tried in the 1960s to provide scholarships for young black cadets, but that offer was declined. Like so much else in the evolution of race relations in our country, VMI followed in due course to do the right thing, but I confess to some frustration that it took so long, and I take great satisfaction that the Jonathan Daniels Humanitarian Award represents the progress of my alma mater toward achieving the noble ideals the drafters of the Constitution had in mind when they adopted the words in the Preamble: "a more perfect union." The award was presented to President Jimmy Carter in 2001 and to former United Nations Ambassador Andrew Young in 2006. In 2004, as part of the remodeling of the institute's barracks, VMI erected an arch in Daniels' memory and engraved it with words from his valedictory address: "I wish you the joy of a purposeful life. I wish you new worlds and the vision to see them. I wish you the decency and nobility of which you are capable. These will come with maturity, which it is now our job to acquire on far-flung fields."

The point of this story is to present an understanding of the institutional process and the time it took for VMI to recognize the fundamental issue that Jonathan Daniels gave his life for. But at least it has happened, and today race is almost irrelevant at VMI, even though unfortunately some black cadets have told me privately that they still feel discrimination. There's much yet to do in our society, as some members of a delegation from VMI learned not that long ago. I accompanied several representatives of VMI in August of 2005, to attend the dedication of a memorial to Jonathan Daniels where he died 40 years before, at the town of Hayneville in Lowndes County, Alabama. Not all the natives of Hayneville were pleased with visitors who came to celebrate the life and death of an "outside agitator." For two of our members, it was the first time they had personally encountered the de facto segregation that exists in places like Lowndes County. One told me that trip was "a life-changing experience," because it was so different from what they thought the reality of society is today.

No experience provided me a clearer illustration of how community action can guide disparate elements of society to seek racial harmony than the Henry Street Project in Roanoke. A once-vibrant social and cultural center for Roanoke African-Americans in the early and mid-20th century, the once-thriving Henry Street commercial district was decaying in the late 1960s from aggressive urban renewal to eradicate officially designated blighted residential areas. Efforts to revitalize the district just beyond the central downtown area were frustrated by hard economics as well as the painful divisions that required healing old wounds inflicted by the lingering effects of segregation. The Henry Street Project slowly, with numerous bumps and bruises along the way, began to bring new life to the district with its proud legacy.

By the mid-1980s, reconciling the divergent strains as a result of urban renewal and its aftermath remained a lingering source of pressure for those community leaders seeking avenues for cooperation. At a TAP board meeting one day in 1986, board member Hazel Thompson told me that the city had plans to demolish her old school — Harrison School, built in 1916 and the first public black high school in the Roanoke Valley. She asked me to help preserve the old building and perhaps restore it for other uses, so we went to Noel Taylor, Roanoke's black mayor, and asked him for his help. We approached a developer, who was well versed in the procedures of obtaining federal grants to provide low-income housing. Eventually, the top floors were converted to apartments for low-income elderly residents, and the ground floor became a community center. My wife Shirley and I then offered to donate some art we had acquired on a number of trips to Africa, including some masks and Benin bronzes. In a short time, the administrators of the community center decided to change its name to the Harrison Museum of African-American Art, which still serves the community today. Soon, with the opening of the new, modern building of the Art Museum of Western Virginia, Harrison is moving downtown into that more extensive space of Center in the Square, continuing to build on the roots of culture and history and providing a reminder of a diverse society's common linkages. Its mission will continue: "to research, preserve and interpret the achievements of African-Americans, specifically in Southwestern Virginia, and to provide an opportunity for all citizens to come together in appreciation, enjoyment and greater knowledge of African-American culture."

These efforts at revitalization in Roanoke continue, still not without occasional friction. For instance, the recent restoration of a pedestrian bridge over the railroad tracks and dedication of a statue of Martin Luther King Jr. did not go without some local controversy — now mostly resolved. The community has come to terms with the bridge and statue as symbols of trying to close the old divide between white downtown Roanoke and black Henry Street. But the extended, good-faith effort on the part of several segments of the community provides a hopeful prospect that Henry Street represents the fulfillment of King's dream for a final end to the racial divisions that deprive all people of fulfilling their common hopes and destinies. As he said in his "I Have a Dream" speech of Aug. 28, 1963, "I have a dream that one day this nation will rise up and live out the true meaning of its creed: We hold these truths to be self evident, that all men are created equal."

Another example of how one thing leads to another is the role of the Oliver Hill Foundation, which my wife Shirley and I helped to start. We raised funds in Oliver Hill's memory to purchase his boyhood home on Gilmer Avenue in Roanoke, close to Henry Street. Washington and Lee Law School saw an opportunity for further outreach and community involvement for its law students, so they are using that house to supplement legal aid work for low-income and elderly people who need legal services in our community.

Such elusive ideals go back to the basic principles of racial and social justice as outlined, but not fully enforced, in our founding documents: the Declaration of Independence and the Constitution. I think our society is trying to promote equal opportunity, but there is so much more to be done.

With each year that passes, we all should ask whether this year will be the one when we determine the need for much-needed renewal of America's commitment to justice, fairness and the rule of law. Indeed, the answer is up to us. We cannot rely on the wisdom or courage of a divided political leadership to provide unerring guidance. We cannot count on the simple passage of time to heal the damage. We have to take matters into our own hands and make the defense of freedom for everyone our own highly personal mission where we live: at the local level.

Chapter Seven

Peace/Human Rights/American Values:
We're All in This Together

Cabell Brand and former Costa Rican President Oscar Arias
and Nobel Peace Prize winner

In his acceptance of the Nobel Peace Prize in 2007, Al Gore quoted an African proverb: " 'If you want go quickly, go alone. If you want to go far, go together.' We need to go far quickly. That means adopting principles, values, laws and treaties that release creativity and initiative at every level of society, in multiple responses originating concurrently and spontaneously." Then Gore added: "When we unite for a moral purpose that is manifestly good and true, the spiritual energy that is released can transform us."

Laureates of the Nobel Peace Prize in recent years reflect an evolving sense about the nature and constitution of peace. Originally the prizes were bestowed on individuals or organizations directly seeking to bring about peace as an end in itself. In later years, the premises for granting the award have expanded its context. Now the criteria include the effects of individual or organizational influences on such disparate areas as environmentalism, as demonstrated by Gore in 2007 for his *An Inconvenient Truth* documentary and Wangari Maathai in 2004 for the beneficial effects of her work in planting trees in Kenya. Other frames of reference include efforts to relieve suffering, especially among refugees of natural or man-made disasters, by organizations such as the Red Cross and Doctors Without Borders. The prizes have expanded to the field of food and education with the recognition in 1970 of Norman Borlaug, who also was involved with George Mitchell and me in the Houston Area Research Center. Inspirational leaders such as Jimmy Carter, Martin Luther King, the Dalai Lama and Muhammad Yunus are also human rights activists. In addition, the Nobel committee recognized personal suffering in the pursuit of peace and an end to such suffering by those such as Nelson Mandela and Eli Wiesel. For providing prudent, creative use of sound international business principles to bring hope to the poor of the world, the prize went to such leaders as Muhammad Yunus and the Grameen Bank in 2006. Before him, in 1953, George Marshall received the prize for his role in the massive reconstruction of Western Europe after World War II in recognition of his leadership first in winning the war and then in securing the peace by ensuring the recovery.

No one should forget those who were recognized through the Nobel Prize in spite of their less-than-successful efforts: Yasser Arafat, Shimon Peres and Anwar Sadat. Peace is never easy, nor is it inevitable. There can be no enduring peace without dramatic efforts to reduce poverty, create meaningful economic activity, educate the public, provide health care for all, sustain our planet through environmental safeguards and ensure justice by safeguarding human rights — by making room for everyone in our global society. If the world is to progress, peace is essential.

Stop for a minute and think what your life would be like if you were trying to live in Afghanistan today. I'm not talking about whether we should be in Afghanistan. Just think about being a citizen of that country with the war raging and terrorist attacks daily. Tens of thousands of Afghan citizens have been killed and even more have been wounded. You can't run a business or schools or hospitals. Life comes to a screeching halt.

I saw this in Europe, as I fought with the U.S. Army through France and Germany. In the aftermath of that destruction, I saw how war itself stopped everything in those societies, and how long those peoples struggled to regain normal lives. The same was true but in even more dire terms in August of 1945, while I was in the European theater and received the news about the atomic bombing of Hiroshima and Nagasaki. Those two events ushered in a grim chapter in human history, the consequences of which not only linger in my memory but also pose new perils today in the form of terrorist threats to acquire and use weapons of mass destruction against innocent civilian populations.

Just suppose you lived in Gaza or Lebanon, in Afghanistan, Iraq, or Sudan, where terrorism is a norm of everyday life. I remember that we used to say that World War I was the war to end all wars. Instead, while it destroyed a dictatorship temporarily and reversed some aggression, it did not deal with the fundamental problems that started that war. Unfortunately, there are just as many wars going on today as we've ever had, some of them at the hands of ruthless dictators against their own subjects, some terrorist waves fomented by religious extremism, many of them rooted in ethnic violence.

My experience in Europe allowed me to understand the importance of business, economic development and the work that Jean Monet envisioned, which evolved from the creation of the coal/steel pool after World War II. Monet's conception of a "common market" was the predecessor to the modern version of the European Union. That political and economic structure creating common ownership of resources and expansion of international trade has essentially prevented the recurrence of multiple wars between France and Germany and other European countries. Unfortunately, the tragedies of war have continued elsewhere: Armed conflicts continue to rage today in different parts of the world. We lived through the tragedy of the Vietnam War, and now Iraq and Afghanistan pose for the United States a challenge in the face of continuing violence in the Middle East, even as violence extends its grim toll to the peoples of Asia, Africa and parts of Latin America. Whatever the rationale and justification for the armed conflicts of the past, the modern era's capability to proliferate weapons of mass destruction further endangers the civilized world.

A major campaign issue of President Obama was to stop the war in Iraq, in which he has made considerable progress with the withdrawal of most American troops. But he also had to wrestle with increasing troops in Afghanistan. As an example of what citizens can do in letting our leaders know how we feel, I've included in Appendix 3 a letter that I wrote to the president after conferring with a large number of people who influenced this important decision.

I take personal satisfaction that, although he did not take my advice completely, he has implemented many of the points and strategies I've suggested.

It's interesting to me that the greatest advocates for peace have been great military leaders who have experienced the horrors of war. Gen. George Marshall won the Nobel Peace Prize for the Marshall Plan after he was the leader of the Allies that won World War II. Gen. Dwight D. Eisenhower, who led the invasion of Western Europe and saw the tragedy of lost lives and then became president for two terms, said it all in 1953 at the end of the Korean War: "Every gun that is made, every warship launched, every rocket fired signifies, in the final sense, a theft from those who are hungry and are not fed, those who are cold and are not clothed. The world in arms is not spending money alone. It is spending the sweat of laborers, the genius of its scientists, the hopes of its children.... This is not a way of life at all, in any true sense. Under the cloud of threatening war, it is humanity hanging from an iron cross."

Eisenhower wisely warned of the threats against civil society by an overweening military-industrial complex. A prudent society should be skeptical of a disproportionate expenditure of the national treasure on the war-making powers at the expense of such common values as education, environmental protection, health care and other aspects of the general welfare. Just as the nation's earliest writers like Thomas Paine defined the promise of the American experiment, we also see in a variety of our common national aspirations the need to secure the peace if justice and human rights are to triumph over chaos and violent conflict.

America's own former political leaders continue to urge a more assertive embrace of the nation's foundational values in navigating the uncertainties of a changing world order. In a recent dialogue with

Public Broadcasting System host Charlie Rose, former U.S. senators Sam Nunn and William Cohen discussed the role of America in the 21ˢᵗ century, emphasizing that the public needs to mold our leaders, restore American leadership and lead as an example for the rest of the world. President Carter in his 2005 book *Our Endangered Values: America's Moral Crisis*, points out that our credibility is in question as a nation that stands for freedom and democracy. We were no longer looked up to in the world, he said, but rather looked down upon. This trend led to terrorism, a pre-emptive war culture in the Bush administration and the forsaking of basic values, including caring for the environment and the poor. In today's world, I share the view of those who say we cannot have peace globally until we finally establish a framework for peace and security in the Middle East.

Again, the benefit of freeing ourselves from reliance on fossil fuels will not only help solve our critical environmental issues of climate change, but will help enormously in political and economic terms by freeing us from the dependence on oil from the Middle East.

My interest in that particular region goes back many years, when my wife and I had the opportunity to visit Israel about 90 days before the Six Day War in 1967 and then again 90 days after the war was over. We later took our children to the Holy Land for Christmas Eve services in Bethlehem and to spend time at a Jewish kibbutz and with the Arabs in the Negev. I think it's important for everyone, especially young people, to know the history of this region. The Middle East is a crucial place to start for us to understand the history that has marked the development of the tensions and tragedies that persist there and that have influenced Islamic militancy worldwide.

Forging a renewed commitment to peace will require of the American people a rediscovery of the fundamental principles that guided the conception of our republic. The Constitution requires that the United States may engage in war only through a declaration by Congress. We the people elect our representatives, so peace can start only when we elect leaders who will represent the values and principles that truly serve the ends of peace and not merely the exertion of military might in ways that invite condemnation from other nations for what they view as aggressive, self-serving overreach.

Former President Jimmy Carter tried to articulate just such a return to basic American principles in his 2002 acceptance address at the presentation of the Nobel Peace Prize: "The world has had ample evidence that war begets only conditions that beget further war. We must remember that today there are at least eight nuclear powers on Earth, and three of them are threatening to their neighbors in areas of great international tension. War may sometimes be a necessary evil, but no matter how necessary, it is always evil, never a good. We will not learn how to live together in peace by killing each other's children. The bond of our common humanity is stronger than the divisiveness of our fears and prejudices. God gives us the capacity for choice. We can choose to alleviate suffering. We can choose to work together for peace. We can make these changes, and we must."

Among the most important practical adjustments the United States can make is for its citizens to reassess the missteps, failures in judgment and abandonment of its constitutional principles to determine where the nation has lost its way in relation to many countries of the world community. America should resume its role as a leading light for other nations, proving that it can lead by example rather than "enforce" by virtue of its economic and military power.

In any event, the United States would serve its own best interests by recognizing the fact of its growing dependence on foreign energy sources. America should acknowledge that dependence and construct a strategy to reduce it through development of alternative energy sources, and in the meantime through treaties to share the resources that are available now. Equally important, the American people should awaken to the historical error of blundering into the invasion of Iraq which, never really was a nation until the British, in their imperialist fashion, divided the Middle East. That was the modus operandi of that era's imperialism, just as, with the help of Germany, Belgium and France, they divided up Africa without regard to ethnic and historical boundaries. What the United States has done is to adopt an imperialist strategy ourselves, which repeats the tragic legacy of the 17th, 18th and 19th centuries. We need leaders who understand what Jeffrey Sachs said in his new book, *Common Wealth: Economics for a Crowded Planet*, that today's global crises are different from the past and require different solutions.

Such is the position of author and *New York Times* columnist Thomas Friedman, who wrote in a column in May of 2008, "I am convinced that the big foreign policy failure that will be pinned on this administration is not the failure to make Iraq work, as devastating as that has been. It will be one with much broader balance of power implications, the failure after 9/11 to put in place an effective energy policy."

I think Friedman was referring to the fact that our leaders should have recognized that each of the terrorists involved in 9/11 was from the Arab world, where more than 50 percent of the oil reserves is located, and on which virtually every country in the world is dependent for its economic security. In the immediate aftermath of Sept. 11, 2001, the world, almost without exception, stood by the United States and was looking for our leadership to do what was necessary to deal with the tragedy of 3,100 Americans who were killed. This is not to say that this criminal act should not have been punished by going after Osama bin Laden and his cohorts in the hills of Afghanistan and Pakistan, but it does say that we had an opportunity with support from throughout the world to deal with the root cause of this terrorist act and marshal the resources and will to prevent a recurrence.

I share the belief that America's highest ideals are precious and that, if Americans and their leaders live by them, the rest of the world will seek to participate in the true freedom and quality embodied in liberal democracy. Such is the same point made by Fareed Zakaria in his book, *The Post-American World*: "America has succeeded not because of the ingenuity of its government programs but because of the vigor of its society. It has thrived because it has kept itself open to the world to goods and services, to ideas and inventions, and above all to people and cultures. This openness has allowed us to respond quickly and flexibly to new economic times, to manage change and diversity with remarkable ease and to push forward the boundaries of individual freedom and autonomy. It has allowed America to create the first universal nation, a place where people from all over the world can work, mingle, mix and share in a common dream and a common destiny."

Developing nations — especially China, India, Brazil and Mexico — aspire to achieve the material benefits enjoyed in the United States, though not necessarily with identical social and political systems. Consequently, the pressure on the world's resources intensifies each year. As Bill McKibben points out in his book, *Deep Economy*, China alone at current rates of development and consumption will theoretically achieve economic parity with the United States by 2031. On its current path, China would then consume the equivalent of two-thirds of the world's entire 2004 grain harvest, 90 million barrels of oil a day, which is 20 million more than current the world demand, and more steel than all of the West combined. "Trying to meet that kind of demand," McKibben wrote, "would stretch the Earth past its breaking point in an almost endless number of ways."

We need to make some fundamental choices about resource allocation and the very principle of growth itself. While the population of the world is still growing, our resources are not, even though we will develop increased efficiencies. Everything in American society is built on the premise of growth. Even in the free-enterprise system itself and the U.S. stock market, investors look for stocks in companies that will grow, that will increase earnings and the value of investments. But demand for energy and commodities, including foodstuffs, are exceeding the global markets' capacity to supply. History tells us that most wars have started because of competition for territory and resources, and too often as a result of religious differences in the quest for power. Building bridges of mutual respect and accommodation will be essential to overcome the swelling suspicions and animosities of the developing countries against the dominance of the developed industrial nations. For instance, establishing global systems for equitable access to the essential resources would go far to blunt the appeal made by some religious extremists. In fact, gathering the array of world leaders and organizations into an alliance to advance the cause of religious harmony is high among priorities for the United Nations and many non-governmental organizations around the world.

"It is urgent," wrote Dr. Heather Eaton of St. Paul University in Ottawa, "for religions to reclaim that the beauty and elegance of the natural world have been inspirational and revivatory of the divine since time immemorial. Human beings have never destroyed that which they considered to be sacred." Member states in the United Nations are recognizing that religious traditions hold the key to peace and security, or that ultimately the misuse and misunderstanding of religion can incite violence and bring chaos to the world. Stressing the urgency of such initiatives, Hilario G. Davide, permanent representative of the Philippines to the United Nations, said, "The partnership between and among governments, the United Nations system, and the religious NGOs and faith communities is no longer an option but a necessity."

Failure to assume that responsibility carries with it inescapable consequences. Consider Iraq, regardless of the merits of the decision by U.S. officials to launch the invasion. The result is that we have destroyed that country, endangered our own fiscal stability and contributed to many thousands of deaths and broken lives, even as we neglected our society's needs at home. In the final analysis, that effort has had little long-term effect on terrorism, and in my view the only way to defeat terrorism is to restore the promise of America, offering the world a massive recommitment to justice, true freedom and equal protection of law. The American people must speak up to our elected leaders to better define our basic goals, consistent with those ideals of freedom and justice for all. Most of the world yearns for that, I believe, and would respond favorably to our leadership in reaffirming them. To do that, though, this nation must do more than give mere lip service to understanding and preserving the highest standards of human rights.

Hundreds of organizations work toward peace and conflict resolution. My essential premise for this book has been to urge problem solving by thinking globally and acting locally. We had a remarkable intern at the Cabell Brand Center in July 2001, who indexed the Web pages of peace organizations and institutions. Jude Leitten, our intern, wrote in the introduction to the bibliography, "We recognize that peace is multi-dimensional, having economic, social, political and cultural implications, and that there are many issues to be resolved. Chief among these include political and racial divisions, health issues, territorial conflicts and religious differences. The hope is that this bibliography will be a foundational source linking all the organizations together on these issues in their common goal: international peace."

A continuing goal of the Cabell Brand Center, and me personally, is the pursuit of peace, which is why the last chapter in the book is devoted to that issue.

Currently, we're in the process of updating Jude Leittner's http://www.ifnotmethenwho.org/Peace.html report on the peace organizations around the world that are dealing with conflict resolution. We've had a number of meetings with the Institute of Peace in Washington at its new facility scheduled to open in 2011. The Institute soon will be able to facilitate these organizations and notable individuals such as all the Nobel Peace Prize winners, which now includes President Obama.

Shirley and I, on a recent trip to Costa Rica, met again with Noble Peace Prize winner President Oscar Arias who is developing a new private conflict resolution center.

Other global organizations are advancing similar, if more modest, initiatives. Among these is the Rotary Club with its foundation that sponsors the Rotary conflict resolution education program, which has identified six universities around the world where their students study for two years.

Other colleges like Eastern Mennonite University in Harrisonburg, Virginia, is teaching conflict resolution, and its alumni all over the world can work together with these other organizations.

Basically, much of my life has been spent in networking and trying to work together for common goals. There is no bigger issue than peace, and no cause is more noble than to have these and other organizations, together with a global grassroots movement of people, work to stop wars and to resolve grave disputes other than by killing.

Each of us can become involved in such activities right away, helping to accelerate the process of understanding the past, acting in the present but recognizing that the first step toward peace in the world requires individuals willing to make that decision, one person at a time. In the lyrics of that lovely song, only the individual can make the solitary choice: "Let there be peace on Earth, and let it begin with me." In that spirit, my wife Shirley and I have been fortunate to participate in the founding of the United Nations Peace University in Costa Rica, and have continued this relationship. We joined the activities of the United Religions Initiative, which is a global, grassroots, interfaith movement to build cultures of peace, justice and healing through a unique organizing model called Cooperation Circle. In addition, after serving eight years on the board I have continued to participate in the Carnegie Council for Ethics and International Policy, which evaluates current "hot button" issues such as the correlation between the environment, health and long-standing questions of war, including children in conflict, refugees, the rights of non-combatants and the role of torture.

I have been blessed to serve with a number of other national organizations in what I call the "interdisciplinary search for peace." I believe this definition reflects the multifaceted dimensions of human endeavor that come to bear on the advance not just of our own American society but also on the complex array of societies that share our common planetary home. Service with the U.S. Chamber of Commerce, the Conference Board, the Carnegie Center for Ethics and Human Rights, the Heinz Center focusing on environmental issues, and the United Nations Development Program introduced me to those diverse aspects of living in harmony as both local and global communities. My work with U.N. projects in Bangladesh and India to encourage economic development in destitute societies was especially instructive in revealing both the potential for good and the potential perils of neglecting the pursuit of peace.

So much of my life has been influenced by experiencing two profoundly ethical decisions by the United States after World War II: the rebuilding of Europe through the Marshall Plan and the courageous resistance against tyranny that broke the Soviet blockade through the Berlin airlift. My good fortune to have participated personally in those horrible conflicts was inspiring evidence to me of the enduring value of struggling to safeguard human rights. With so many conflicts erupting around the world, seeking peaceful resolutions should remain our uncompromising ethical mandate as a people.

No economic development, no positive activities, can take place without peace. Peace must become the universal given. With peace, life, hope, dreams and work for a better life all become possible. With war, everything comes to a screeching halt, and inhumanity prevails.

Anglican Archbishop Desmond Tutu knows with painful certainty the cost of violence after his historic role in helping to abolish the injustice of apartheid in South Africa. Tutu received the Nobel Peace Prize in 1984, a full decade before that country ended the legal segregation of blacks from the civic life of the former British-ruled African nation. Persisting against racism and inflexible political opposition from the white establishment, Tutu provided a courageous example of determined commitment to justice and human rights as the prerequisite conditions for peace to exist. "Peace without justice is an impossibility," Tutu said. "If we could but recognize our common humanity, that we do belong together, that our destinies are bound up in one another's, that we can be free only together, that we can survive only together, that we can be human only together, then a glorious world will come into being where all of us lived harmoniously together as members of one family, the human family."

As critical as addressing global tensions and conflict may be, dispute-resolution first must begin at home. The periodic emergence of hate groups in the United States reflects the consequences of failing to incorporate such principles basic to democracy. A major goal of the Institute for Peace Educational Center in Washington, D.C., is to teach school children these ideals of conflict-resolution.

Richard Solomon, CEO on the U.S. Institute of Peace in Washington D.C. with Cabell Brand

All of this underscores the basic premise I have sought to advance, which is the imperative of local involvement. Each of us has an opportunity to be involved in a variety of local organizations and activities that promote the values outlined in just the chapter titles of this book. We can help protect the planet with environmental activism. We can stop wasting resources. We can promote human rights and the opportunity for everyone to have a better future. We can deal with poverty locally and globally by helping to bring fresh water to those in need — increasingly a challenging threat as the oceans rise. None of this will happen without local involvement. I conclude with my wish: That each person who chooses to read this book, if you're lucky enough to live as long and as fruitful life as I have, will feel as good as I do about the work that I've tried to do locally. These efforts in turn have opened new vistas onto opportunities to engage national and global challenges, with the ultimate goal of trying to give everyone in the world a better life as we protect the planet itself.

In the end, we *are* all in this together.

"No one can do everything, but everyone can do something."
— Austin Cloyd
Quote used by the American Red Cross Celebration of Hero's Award
Given to Cabell Brand.

Credits

Hundreds of people along the way have helped me in everything that I've been able to do, and I thank them all. Six particular people have had a major part in the development of this book, and I wish to give special credit to them, because I would not have been able to write this book without it.

Tommy Denton is my co-author. I was fortunate to have Tommy as a friend when he retired as editorial page editor of *The Roanoke Times*. I would like to pay tribute to Tommy for his help, his understanding, his perspective, and his ability to take rambling words from dictation and put them into coherent sentences.

Alecia Nash and her computer company have helped me with my computer skills for the last several years. In this day and age of e-books, e-mails and the use of the computer itself, I could not have produced this book without her able assistance in many ways beyond just the computer.

Jessica Mowles, a young college graduate, has helped me for the last few years on a part-time basis. With Alecia Nash's help, Jessica has put together my scrapbooks in sequence from random files I've kept of activities I've had in my life. These scrapbooks were invaluable for reference.

Ted Edlich, president of Total Action Against Poverty (TAP) and to whom I refer often in the book, has written the epilogue relating our experiences together. Without his leadership and counsel — and most definitely because of our deep, abiding friendship — I could not have begun to do the things I recount in this book.

Harlan Beckley, the founder and head of the Shepherd Program for the Interdisciplinary Study of Poverty and Human Capability at Washington and Lee, affirmed my hope that this book could be an inspiration to young college graduates. He also has written an introduction. His counsel and editing skills also have been of enormous benefit.

Davis Masten, chairman of the Presidents Circle of the National Academy of Sciences, and Ralph Cicerone, president of the National Academies, each encouraged me along the way. With their advice, they have contributed greatly to this book.

A History of the Cabell Brand Center

The history of the Cabell Brand Center is reported on its web page at www.cabellbrandcenter.org. But, briefly, it was established in 1986 by Cabell Brand and Roanoke College to give students there and in nearby colleges an opportunity to study poverty and environmental issues. Over 500 fellowships have been awarded with funds coming from volunteer contributions.

The Center was managed for nearly 20 years by Nineveh Wygal who died in 2008 after having worked for Cabell Brand for 54 years. The Center had been managed earlier by Dave Herbert and Martin Skelly, now by David Crawford of Rainwater Management Solutions.

When the Center was relocated from Roanoke College, the Poverty Library was given to Washington and Lee University, the Environmental Library was divided between Roanoke College and The Roanoke Higher Education Center, the Stuart McGuire history was deposited in the Roanoke College archives, and Cabell Brand's personal memoirs are in the Virginia Military Institute archives.

Today the center's focus continues to be poverty, the environment, and peace. On environmental issues, we're using the shortage of fresh water as an example of local action by saving rain water, storing it for productive use, and establishing ways further to reduce storm-drain runoff. The shortage of drinking water is a critical problem for the world today and has fostered conflicts in many areas, even in the United States. This problem will be multiplied as the oceans rise and as dislocation of millions of people intensifies in coastal areas.

As I write, the current estimates are that within 100 years the oceans will rise much more than 1 meter. This puts areas such as Bangladesh, which rests only 1 foot above sea level, in desperate straits.

All of the income from the sale of this book goes into the non-profit Cabell Brand Center to promote and work on these specific issues. There are a number of scholarship opportunities currently available through our center. Please see our web site for more information at **http://www.ifnotmethenwho.org/Scholarship.html.**

Families in Transition ◆ Head Start ◆ Housing & Community Development
TAP Financial Services ◆ This Valley Works

Epilogue

By: Dr. Ted Edlich

President, Total Action Against Poverty

I have known Cabell Brand since 1965. At that time I was a young Presbyterian Minister in Buchanan, Virginia, a small town in the county of Botetourt, Virginia. I had recently completed a fellowship at Yale Divinity School in social and political ethics. The issue of poverty had broken on the American agenda with the publication of *The Other America* by Michael Harrington and the launching of the War on Poverty by Lyndon Johnson in the wake of the assassination of President Kennedy.

At that time Cabell was organizing community meetings throughout the Roanoke Valley including the county of Botetourt where I was pastor of two churches. It was my privilege to assist in the organization of one of the community meetings in my county that contributed to the development of TAP in the Roanoke Valley.

Little did I know then how my life would be entwined and come under the influence of Cabell and Shirley Brand and their entire family. As TAP was created, it was clear to me that the church needed to collaborate with an organization that was committed to the "least of these my brethren" and so as I became the Director of an urban ministry in Roanoke with eleven Presbyterian churches, we fully collaborated with the growing antipoverty organization that Cabell had inspired. I joined the TAP staff in 1968 as the second Head Start Director and was privileged to become TAP's CEO in 1975.

In the Roanoke Valley of Southwest Virginia, our little piece of the universe, Cabell is a legend. John Hancock, the President of Roanoke Electric Steel whose political dominance was such that the governor of Virginia, whether Republican or Democrat, never failed to come to his

Christmas party, once confided, "Cabell Brand was ahead of all of us with respect to race relations and the importance of dealing with the issue of poverty."

Yet Cabell's vision and impact have always been on a larger scale. Sergeant Shriver, the first Director of the Peace Corps, the first Director of the Office on Economic Opportunity, and with his wife Founder of the Special Olympics, once remarked, "Cabell, if we had had four businessmen such as yourself, we would have won the War on Poverty!"

It was my privilege to help facilitate a planning session for the leadership of the National Direct Selling Association that included the presidents of Avon, Amway, and others of that stature. Cabell Brand stood out among his contemporaries as the brightest and best. Cabell's intellect, his focus, his business acumen, his determination to make a difference made Cabell not only a big fish in a small pond but a big fish in any pond that he chose to swim in.

During my seventy years, I have been privileged to know many business, community, religious and political leaders across the United States. I have never met any one who considers the gift of life more precious and is more dedicated to making his life count in building a more just and strong America, a more sustainable planet, and a future of opportunity for all of the world's children. Cabell and I have seldom talked religion. Cabell does not waste time talking religion; he lets his actions speak his commitment about the sanctity of life.

I have been the pastor without portfolio to the Brand Family. I have helped to bury Brand children way before their time. I have seen Cabell and Shirley, and their children, in the best of times and the worst of times. Yet no matter the pain and sorrow, their commitment to making this a better world has never wavered.

Cabell is so intentional about life that he has a yearly plan for himself, his family, and his work for the society. Just being around Cabell forces you to adopt the same strategy. If you do not have enough plans for yourself, Cabell will be all too willing to assist you. A colleague of ours, Wilma Warren, who was instrumental in developing the Virginia Water Project which became the National Demonstration Water Project, once told Cabell, "Cabell, I can only meet with you once every six months because it takes that long for me to complete what you asked me to do in our last meeting!"

I hope that you will learn a number of things from this book. I hope that you will be inspired to be concerned about the cancer of poverty in our society that robs our society of the talent, the capital, and the social resources to make America a leader for the future. I hope that you will be inspired to love this precious planet as Cabell does and work for sustainable communities throughout the world. Above all I hope that you will love your own life with the same visceral appreciation that Cabell has for every breath he takes and every thought he is able to contemplate and to dare to make the most of this precious gift of life God has given you.

During the revolutionary sixties of the last century, the watchword was, "If you are not part of the solution, then you are part of the problem!" Read this book. Enlarge your vision. Think globally; act locally. Change the world. Be part of the solution.

Ted Edlich, TAP President

Cabell Brand

GENERAL INFORMATION

Chairman - Cabell Brand Center for International Poverty & Resource Studies

Web Site: www.CabellBrandCenter.org or www. IfNotMeThenWho.org

He is married to the former Shirley Hurt and together they have five children and 13 grandchildren.

EDUCATIONAL BACKGROUND

- Graduated from Andrew Lewis High School, Salem, VA - 1940 (Most Outstanding Student).

- Editor of high school newspaper and on state championship debating team for three years.

- Graduated from Virginia Military Institute (VMI) - 1944 (first in class in Electrical Engineering).

- Attended nine sessions at Harvard Business School, and University of Virginia in conjunction with special programs of the Young Presidents' Organization.

- Completed AMA Management Course and AMA's President's Course.

MILITARY SERVICE

- U.S. Army for four years - World War II, 70th Infantry Division, European Theatre; received the Bronze Star; held rank of Captain at end of military service.

WORK HISTORY - CURRENT

- Founder & Chairman – Cabell Brand Center for International Poverty and Resource Studies – 1988 to Present

- Shepherd Poverty Program Alumni-Advisory Committee

at Washington & Lee University - 1999 to Present

- Director for the Foundation for Alternative and Integrative Medicine - 2005 to Present
- Advisor to the President of Lynchburg College on matters of natural resource use, economics, and public service - 2010 to Present

WORK HISTORY - PREVIOUS

- Economic Analyst in the Intelligence Office of Berlin Military Government (in Berlin during The Blockade) and with the U.S. Foreign Service in Europe - 1947 to 1949
- Vice President - The Ortho-Vent Shoe Co. - 1949 to 1962
- President - Brand-Edmonds Associates Advertising - 1956 to 1966
- Chairman of the Board - Brand-Edmonds Associates Advertising -1962 to 1981
- Founder and President - The Stuart McGuire Company, Inc. - 1962 to1985
- Chairman of the Board & Chief Executive Officer - The Stuart McGuire Co., Inc. - 1973 to 1986
- Chairman Emeritus - The Stuart McGuire Co., Inc. (assumed Sales Manager position at Ortho-Vent Shoe Co. - 1949; developed Direct Selling shoe business into a national corporation; taking it public in 1970 as The Stuart McGuire Co.; expanded product line to ready-to-wear and jewelry; converted to a mail order conglomerate, then into a full service mall order operations and fulfillment business. Finally merged corporation in 1986 with Home Shopping Network.)
- Consultant - Home Shopping Network - 1986 to 1995
- Board of Directors - First Virginia Bank- Southwest Roanoke, VA. (Successor to Farmers National Bank of Salem, VA.) - 1973 to 1997
- Board of Directors - First Virginia Banks

Inc., Falls Church, VA. -1976 to 1997

- Board of Directors - Interstate Engineering
  Co, Anaheim, CA. – 1996 – 2002
    - Electrolux Corporation 1996 - 2003
    - Armstrong Chemical 1981 – 1990
- President - Recovery Systems, Inc. – 1986 - 2004 main
  business - international sustainable environmental
  and economic development consultants
- Research Associate - Roanoke College – 1986 - 2005

AWARDS & HONORS

- Director of the Young Presidents' Organization 1972
- Hall of Fame Award of the Direct Selling Association
- "Outstanding Citizen Award" by the Virginia
  Council of Social Welfare 1967
- "Distinguished Service Award" by the Roanoke JC's 1975
- "Citizen of the Year" by the Salem Roanoke
  Co. Chamber of Commerce 1979
- VISTA Award (1980 – as the businessman in the U.S.
  who had done the most for low income people)
- Finalist for the "Chivas Regal National
  Entrepreneur Award" 1989
- Virginia State Board of Health (nine years
  – served as Chairman until 1989)
- Lyndon Baines Johnson Humanitarian Award 1990
- Ink Magazine, National Award for
  "Entrepreneur of the Year" 1990
- Humanitarian Award from that National
  Conference of Christians and Jews 1991
- Gold Medal Award from the Governor of Virginia
  Doug Wilder for "Volunteering Excellence" 1992
- Recipient of the first "Jonathan Daniels

Award" by VMI Promaji Club 1992

- Featured in *"Some do Care"* for exemplary leadership in the United States 1993
- "Noel Taylor Humanitarian Award" presented by Senator John Warner 1995
- "John C. Hancock Community Service Award" by the Roanoke United Way 1996
- "Award of Excellence" by the Clean Valley Council 1997
- South West Virginia Junior Achievement Hall of Fame 1997
- Received Honorary Degree as Doctor of Humane Letters from Roanoke College May 1997
- Featured in *"Stone Soup for the World"* along with Eleanor Roosevelt, President Jimmy Carter , and Nelson Mandela 1998
- "Outstanding Citizen's Award" Salem Rotary Club 1999
- Received Honorary Degree as Doctor of Letters from Washington & Lee University June 1999
- Virginia Conservation Network "Lifetime Award for Environmental Activism" 2003
- Received Honorary Degree as Doctor of Humanities from Ferrum College June 2005
- Received an Honorary Degree as Associate in Human Letters from Virginia Western Community College June 2005 where he was also the keynote speaker for the graduation
- First recipient of the Salem-Roanoke County Chamber of Commerce Life time Achievement Award March 30th, 2010
- The American Red Cross Celebration of Heroes Award for Community Impact March 31st, 2010
- The National Society of the Daughters of the American Revolution (DAR) Medal of Honor awarded May 8th, 2010

CIVIC, INDUSTRIAL, VOLUNTEER & PROFESSIONAL AFFILIATIONS

Current

Member	The U.S. Association of the Club of Rome
Member	Social Venture Network
Life Member	Direct Selling Association
Member	Roanoke Valley Historical Society
Member	Torch Club of Roanoke Valley
Member	Shenandoah Club
Member	Salem Presbyterian Church
Member	President's Circle - National Academy of Sciences
Member	Roanoke Valley Business Council
Member	Roanoke and Salem Chambers of Commerce

CIVIC, INDUSTRIAL, VOLUNTEER & PROFESSIONAL AFFILIATIONS

Previous

Founder/ Chairman Emeritus	Total Action Against Poverty in the Roanoke Valley (TAP). Participated in starting this anti-poverty program with business sponsorship and served as its first and only President - 1965 to 1995
Board of Directors	CHIP of Virginia (Child Health Investment Project) - 1992.... Chairman - 1993 to 1996
Member	Virginia State Board of Health - 1984 to 1993 Vice Chairman - 1985 to 1989; Chairman - 1989 to 1993
Board of Directors	ATI/Armstrong Laboratories, West Roxbury, MA. 1987 to 1993
Board of Directors	The Woodlands Center for Growth Studies, a research consortium of Texas Universities (HARC)

Board of Advisors	The Institute of Socioeconomic Affairs, White Plains, NY.
Board of Directors	Global Water, Washington, DC.
Member	Governor's Commission of Federal Funding of State Domestic Program (appointed by Governor Gerald Baliles) - 1986 to 1988
Chairman	World Business Council Argentina Seminar Buenos Aires - 1988
President	Private Sector Commission of Virginia Community Action Agencies - 1986 to 1987
Member	Futures Advisory Board of Congressional Clearinghouse on the Future, Washington, DC. - 1983 to 1987
Member	Commission of Block Grants of the Commonwealth of Virginia (appointed by Governor Charles S. Robb) - 1982 to 1985
Chairman of the Board	Direct Selling Association
Chairman	DSA Long Range Planning Committee
Chairman	Task Force on Employment (and initiated local Business Advisory Council to coordinate resources of business, public schools and government programs in improving job opportunities)
Director	Young Presidents' Organization
Chairman	YPO International Education Committee

Chairman	Chairman of the following YPO Seminars
	• South American Seminar - February 1968
	• Mid-American Seminar - Jan./Feb. 1969
	• White House Fellows (co-chaired) - July 1970
	• Comparative Governments - Sept./Oct. 1970
	• African Seminar - July/August 1971
	• Soviet Union Seminar - July/August 1972
Founding Member and President	Roanoke Touchdown Club
President	Salem Rotary Club
Director	Roanoke Sales Executive Club
Director	Roanoke Valley Council on Community Services
Director	The Ethics Resource Center
Director	Opportunities Industrialization Center (OIC); participated in setting up its vocational training facility in the Roanoke Valley
Trustee	Carnegie Council on Ethics & International Affairs (CCEIA)
Member	Chamber of Commerce of the United States - Education and Manpower Committee; Council on Trends and Perspective
Part-Time Professor	Roanoke College (helped develop Night School; taught courses in business administration and advertising)
Member	Roanoke County School Standards on Education Committee
Member	President's Association of the American Management Association

Founding Member	World Business Academy, Burlingame, CA. - 1987....
Board of Directors	Virginia Community Development Corp., Richmond, VA. – 1992 - 2006
Board of Directors	Virginia Health Care Foundation, Richmond, VA. – 1993 – 2000
Board of Directors	Virginia Foundation for the Humanities and Public Policy, Charlottesville, VA. - 1993. - 1998
Board of Directors	Blue Ridge Public Television – 1993 - 2005
Board of Directors	Action Alliance for Virginia's Children & Youth – 1994 - 2002
Board of Trustees	Western Virginia Land Trust, Roanoke, VA. -1995 – 2003
Associate	World Resources Institute, Washington, DC. – 1985 – 2004
Member	New Century Council Quality of Life/ Environment Committee- 1995 – 2002
Member	Executive Council of The Conference Board, New York, NY.
Member	The Chief Executives Organization (CEO), Bethesda, MD.
Member	World Presidents' Organization, Alexandria, VA.
Member	The Newcomen Society of North America
Formerly Trustee	The H. John Heinz III Center for Science, Economics and the Environment
For Reference see	Who's Who in America

Tommy Denton

PROFESSIONAL EXPERIENCE

- Columnist, *The Roanoke Times*, 2006 to retirement, 2007.

- Editorial Page Editor, *The Roanoke Times*, January 1998 to 2006.

- Senior Editorial Writer and Columnist, *Fort Worth Star-Telegram*, Fort Worth, Texas, January 1991 to January 1998.

- Co-Author, *Why Didn't You Get Me Out?*, with Frank Anton, published, June 1997 by Summit Publishing Group.

- Editorial Page Editor, *Fort Worth Star-Telegram*, Fort Worth, Texas, August 1987 to January 1991.

- Op-Ed Page Editor, *Fort Worth Star-Telegram*, Fort Worth, Texas, May, 1983 to August 1987.

Executive Assistant for State Affairs, U.S. Sen. Lloyd M. Bentsen, managing Senator Bentsen's operations in Texas, January 1981 to April 1983.

- Copy Editor, *The Philadelphia Inquirer*, Philadelphia, Pa., July 1978 to January 1981. Responsible for sports section page makeup and design, copy editing and headline writing.

- Assistant Director, Texas Register Division, Office of the Secretary of State, Austin, Texas, October 1975 to July 1978. Management of compilation and publication of state agency administrative regulations in the *Texas Register*.

- General Assignment Reporter, the *Charlotte News*, Charlotte, N.C., March 1972 to July 1973, covering special assignments, federal court and public education.

- Reporter, *Amarillo Globe-News*, Amarillo, Texas, June 1971 to March 1972, covering special assignments and news features. Employed at the *Globe-News*, May through August 1968 before entering military service.

RECENT PROFESSIONAL AWARDS

- 1999, First Place, column writing, Virginia Press Association.
- 1996, First Place, editorial writing, Associated Press Managing Editors Association of Texas.
- 1995, First Place, editorial writing, Associated Press Managing Editors Association of Texas.
- 1994, First Place, column writing, Associated Press Managing Editors Association of Texas.

ACADEMIC

- Adjunct professor, Honors Program, Virginia Tech University, January through May of 2008.
- Virginius Dabney Distinguished Professorship in Editorial and Column Writing, Virginia Commonwealth University, February through April of 1999.
- Adjunct professor, Department of Journalism, Texas Christian University, teaching upper-level course in opinion writing, fall terms from 1988 through 1997.
- Master of Public Affairs, Lyndon B. Johnson School of Public Affairs, The University of Texas at Austin, May 1975.
- Master of Science in Journalism, Northwestern University, Medill School of Journalism, Evanston, Ill., June 1971.
- Bachelor of Arts, Baylor University, Waco, Texas, May 1968. Attended on academic/athletic scholarship in football, 1964-1968. Letterman.

PROFESSIONAL AFFILIATIONS

- National Conference of Editorial Writers Foundation, president, 2001 to 2004.
- National Conference of Editorial Writers

Foundation, treasurer, 1997 to 2001.

- National Conference of Editorial Writers, president, 1995.

MILITARY SERVICE

- U.S. Army, 196th Light Infantry Brigade, Vietnam, 1969-70.
- As Sergeant E-5, served as leader of an .81 mm mortar squad. Bronze Star.

PERSONAL

Born: October 25, 1945
Married: Jean Louise Frederick, June 10, 1972.
            Son, Zachary McMillan Denton
            Daughter, Elizabeth Anne Denton
            Son, Luke Frederick Denton

Cabell served two years in WWII with the 570th Signal Company of the 70th Infantry Division. This picture was taken France in January of 1945.

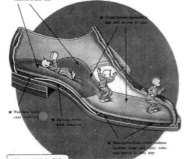

This presentation of the Spring Step Cushion design helped to propel Stuart McGuire's success through door-to-door sales.

This is an example of the semi-annual Stuart McGuire catalogue published for 26 years.

This cover of the Stuart McGuire annual report shows the transition to mail-order marketing.

Stuart McGuire constructed a 250,000 square-foot distribution center that was the home of the Marketechs Division that distributed products for 40 other mail-order companies.

Treasury Secretary William Miller June of 1980 at the Kennedy Canter presented Cabell with the Vista Award for the business man who had done the most to help the nation's poor.

In 1998, Cabell informed President Clinton at the White House of the need to extend the community service block grants to support community action agencies nationwide.

Cabell discussed with Sargent Shriver the progress of community action agencies in Virginia on the White House lawn in 1980.

Cabell presented a display of TAP and Virginia Cares in 1984 at the International Conference on Human Rights in New Delhi, India.

Head Start children enjoyed a friendly conversation with Cabell in Roanoke, Virginia in 1966.

Cabell presided at the 1967 opening of the Head Start Center in Salem, Virginia. Norfolk Southern Railway donated the building that is still in operation today.

Cabell provided insights to Shepherd Program Students about community action agencies in 2007 in Roanoke, Virginia.

During a White House conference in 1998, Vice President Al Gore compared notes with Cabell about administration environmental policies.

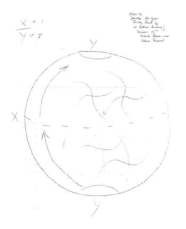

This is a drawling done by Al Gore for Cabell Brand in 1989 illustrating the Gaia Theory.

Cabell Brand with Al Gore in his congressional office in 1979.

The Heinz Center Board of Directors met in 2006 to develop strategies for protecting marine ecology.

Hans Wack, left, received a briefing and demonstration in 2007from Dave and Ed Crawford about Cabell's rainwater harvesting system.

A Virginia Military Institute cadet approaches the arch emblazoned with a quotation from the 1961 valedictory address by Jonathan Daniels.

This image of Jonathan Daniels appears in the Martyrs Chapel of the Canterbury Cathedral, London, England.

Officers of the Promaji Club at VMI presented Cabell with the first Jonathan Daniels Humanitarian Award in 1992.

VMI Superintendent Major General Josiah Bunting with cadet representatives of the Promaji Club unveiled the monument honoring Jonathan Daniels at Hayneville, Alabama, August 23, 1997.

After the dedication of the memorial, visitors marched to Cash's store, where Jonathan Daniels was murdered.

Oliver Hill, seated left, visited with Shirley, Jonathan Stubbs, and Cabell after an Oliver Hill Foundation meeting in 2004.

Former President Carter welcomed delegates from many different religious groups and organizations to discuss the role of religion and world peace in 1999 at the Carter Center Peace Conference in Atlanta.

Roanoke College Student Activities at the Cabell Brand Center for International Poverty and Resource Studies, which opened in 1987.

This is an architect's rendering of the new Institute of Peace when under construction located on Constitution Avenue Washington DC

Appendix 1

Op-Ed Article 3-24-2009:
Cabell Brand's Philosophy on the Financial Crisis

As America teeters at the edge of an economic crisis unseen for 70 years, far too many critical members of the nation's political leadership are exhibiting a frightening degree of negligence, if not civic cowardice.

Millions of Americans are out of work, and millions of others hang precariously in the balance, even as unemployment benefits for many of them are set to expire within the next few weeks.

Forty-seven million people lack health insurance, and that number surely will increase as unemployment worsens. An additional 15 million people are underinsured.

Food banks are emptying, charities are struggling, and no government shows signs of knowing exactly what to do. People have no place to turn. They don't know what to do, either.

I may not be a financial expert, but I've been in business most of the 86 years of my life. I've learned that when there is a breakdown in operations, somebody has to pay the price. Right now, the American people are paying the price for the corrosive disruption of the American economy — indeed, the global economy — that should be set right by the banks and the financial institutions responsible for the grotesque excesses that have caused the economic catastrophe our nation now faces.

The core source of our problem is mortgage securities, unregulated financial instruments such as derivatives and other exotic investment vehicles exploited by many financial institutions, but especially unregulated hedge funds.

The creation and worldwide distribution of those instruments — "protected" by unregulated collateralized debt obligations that mocked any notion of sound insurance— defied the most primary business discipline of prudent risk management. The speculative orgy among unaccountable U.S. financial firms that ensued brought us to this painful pass.

Repairing the damage will require a quick solution. First, let AIG go bankrupt immediately. Obviously, this would have repercussions with all their customers, many of whom are banks, but the basic problem has been the insuring of mortgage-backed securities, which never should have been written in the first place. Somebody has to eat the losses, which could equal more than $2 trillion, and the perpetrators of the damage should do the eating.

Our financial system — as wounded as it may be — can deal with bankruptcy. We can deal with the Federal Deposit Insurance Corporation taking over banks, which might fail with the bankruptcy of AIG, but we should not tolerate the suffering of millions of Americans without doing something immediately to help them by restoring our crippled national economy.

Let the FDIC take over defaulting banks, insure the taxpayer deposits, write down their portfolio of investments and then sell it back to private interests. That would expedite the banks' being back in business, lending money to businesses that need loans to keep operating.

There's no question in my mind that unemployment is going to 10 percent, maybe even 15 percent before things turn around. That statistic means that 30 percent of the American people who want jobs will not be working, because unemployment statistics count only those who are actively looking for jobs, not those who have given up.

But this also means that the majority of the American people are working, many on reduced hours or performing part-time work, but to restore the confidence quickly, somebody has to take charge and absorb the losses caused by the unregulated financial instruments.

The bonus payments at AIG are a smokescreen. It's a minor issue, but it is a symptom of the greed of Wall Street and the way that executives have manipulated the system to their own personal advantage. Many of them have taken their huge profits and run, and are no longer active in business. They are the culprits.

How did all this start? In my opinion, it started in 1980 with the election of Ronald Reagan, who said, "Government is the problem." Since that time, there's been accelerating deregulation, and government has gotten out of the business of protecting the economic interests of the American people.

America experienced eight years of this negligence under Reagan, followed by four years under George H.W. Bush, followed by eight years under Bill Clinton. Now, after eight years of George W. Bush, the country has endured 29 years of building up to the inevitable consequences.

Yet it was Clinton's Democratic Treasury Secretary Robert Rubin who convinced the president in 1999 to agree to repeal of the Glass-Steagall Act. Enacted in 1933, Glass-Steagall responded to the incestuous speculation that led to the Great Depression and was designed to protect the banking system. The law erected firewalls between commercial banks and other financial institutions to prevent the speculative excesses that caused the Great Depression.

Reagan's unrelenting attack on regulation exhibited its first consequences with the savings and loan crisis in the late 1980s. Gradual erosion of regulatory institutions resulted in both the dot-com disaster in 2000-2001 and the current meltdown in mortgage-backed securities we're now experiencing.

Unfortunately, the American public doesn't understand how it happened, when it was happening, or what to do about it. I'm not sure that I know, either, but I do know that our house is burning, and we've got to put out the fire quickly.

The first step, I believe, is to bite the bullet on the mortgage-backed securities, which is the major culprit. William Cohan's recent book, The House of Cards, eloquently explains what happened to the Bear Stearns investment banking firm. Bear Stearns leveraged its holding of mortgage-backed securities, taking overnight funds, borrowing them for the short term, and trying to use as collateral those mortgage-backed securities until private firms would no longer take them. So the firm was left holding the bag with loans it couldn't pay back.

In addition to that scenario, the investment banking firms had insured those sometimes-worthless financial instruments with AIG, because they thought they were good collateral. They had the backing of Moody's and other rating firms, which bear considerable responsibility for the gross irresponsibility of the financial sector, paid as they were for those favorable ratings by the very firms they "evaluated." They, too, were interested in short-term profits and not upholding their responsibility of trust, which they had built up for many years in our society.

The last person to blame for this emergency is President Obama. As I write this, he has been in office for less than two months. He has done a remarkable job in that brief time, putting together a Cabinet in 30 days, passing a stimulus bill immediately, and doing more positively to try to correct a 30-year old problem than any president in history.

My friends know me as a Democrat, which I am, but I am blaming the Republicans for starting the problem. I also, however, am blaming the Democrats and the Clinton administration for continuing it. It's been going on since 1980, and Obama is faced with the daunting challenge of trying to fix it.

The corporate bonuses and the responsibility for huge payments to the greedy financial executives have been going on for years, but the usurpation was institutionalized by George W. Bush and his Treasury Secretary Henry Paulson, who engineered the first bailout in September of 2008. That program contained the provision that under no circumstances would the compensation of the executives be limited by the government, that it was a private matter.

That fostered this bonus question, which Obama has inherited as part of a trillion-dollar federal budget deficit. Add the stimulus and the obligations that the federal government has taken since then, and our budget deficit is even more — and it's growing.

Now the Republicans are complaining that the budget's too big. But what is their plan? How would they fix it? They, after all, were the engineers of the economic train wreck that afflicts the nation now. I've seen no credible, worthwhile alternative to the administration's plan, not even from the Democratic Congress.

My opinion is that these politicians, most of whom are well-intentioned public servants, don't understand the problem, either. I personally am not sure that President Obama and Treasury Secretary Timothy Geithner understand the problem. Geithner may even be part of the problem, because he was part of that system, along with Clinton's Treasury Secretary Lawrence Summers, now Obama's White House economic adviser, and others who continued that process of getting the government out of the regulation business.

For a variety of reasons, Geithner now faces the overwhelming responsibility of trying to administer the Treasury Department with a grossly understaffed bureaucracy. He needs help, but the political liabilities of so many talented people with economic expertise from previous Democratic administrations have caused a reluctance to answer the call to public service because of current political scrutiny.

Geithner and the president should consider turning quickly to senior economists and other experts in the International Monetary Fund and the World Bank, as well as those knowledgeable financial experts who have never had strong ties to the current culture of Wall Street.

Poverty is increasing. Hunger is increasing. Unemployment is increasing. Businesses are contracting. Bankruptcies are increasing. Somebody has to bite the bullet.

Whether Geithner's recent proposal to offer federal guarantees will succeed in attracting private investors to buy the "toxic" assets from banks remains to be seen. No doubt the offending banks are hoping to benefit from a "heads we win, tails you lose" proposition to compensate for their failure to exercise due diligence as they wallowed in the fast-buck dodge of mortgage-back securities in the first place.

In the meantime, those who caused the problem elude responsibility for their actions, hardly a satisfying outcome.

Still, there is clearly a limit to the amount of money that the U.S. Treasury and the Federal Reserve can make available to private industry to bail them out in this economic crisis. Therefore, priorities must be established as to which are the most important elements to repair quickly, increase employment, decrease the pain on the American people and at the same time build the strong financial system with prudently rigorous controls for the future.

As a businessman who has spent the last 60 years observing one federal administration after another, I am very happy that we are fortunate enough to have a president like Obama, whose instincts are right, who is brilliant and well-educated, with no vested interest in anything except the future of the American people.

Whether you agree with me or not is irrelevant, because he is our president for the next four years, and the only way that we will get out of this crisis is for everybody to support the administration and work together to solve the problem — individually and collectively.

Appendix 2

November 20th, 2009
President Barack Obama
The White House
1600 Pennsylvania Avenue NW
Washington, DC 20500

RE: Suggested Afghanistan Policy

Dear Mr. President,

You successfully campaigned against the Iraq War and are doing the best you can to remove our combat troops from Iraq. Thank you.

You also inherited the NATO war in Afghanistan, which is not just a United States war. The original strategy developed eight years ago was to eliminate the Al-Qaida terrorists from that country. This has been done. Reports today show there are less than 100 such terrorists left in Afghanistan.

Times have changed. Thank you for the careful consideration that you are giving to a new strategy.

My suggestion is that you should not make a United States decision on increasing troops to Afghanistan. This is not a United States decision. This should be a NATO decision.

My proposal is that you call for an immediate summit of all NATO nations and invite China, India, and Iran to participate. The problem today in the world is with global terrorism - - groups of fanatics who want to destroy the ways of life in all of the countries listed above. I suggest this summit be held in either London or Madrid, countries who have also suffered terrorist attacks like, our 9-11 tragedy.

Many of the original Afghanistan terrorists are now in Pakistan, but they are also in many other places as proven by their attacks in several other countries. They will go to any country where they can operate to accomplish their goals, including the US, England, Spain, Germany, Somalia, Yemen, and Sudan.

The purpose of the summit is to develop a new global strategy for all countries to work together to eliminate these terrorist organizations. This is a multi-generational problem.

As you know Afghanistan does not have a functional democracy, and never had. The main goal of the people of Afghanistan is basic security and the delivery of fundamental infrastructure services such as water and electricity.

There is no role for combat troops in this effort. We should ask each country to provide large financial resources to help the Afghan people and also other countries such as Pakistan to create functional democracies with basic security and infrastructure.

This bottoms-up strategy must be done by the local people, particularly the Afghans, but it will probably take as much money as we have been spending on combat troops. NATO nations and the other participants of this summit need to help. This must be a coordinated global strategy to fight terrorism wherever it arises. And this program needs to be reviewed and revised regularly as conditions change.

Far from a retreat, this is an aggressive positive program with a long range goal to develop the core ingredients for peace, security, and free enterprise, with respect everywhere for human rights.

We must show the world that this is the way to live.

This global cooperative effort for peace can also be used to help the necessary movements on critical environmental issues and the reduction of global poverty.

As we develop this strategy, you can use your skills first in negotiation and secondly in explaining this to the American people.

Sincerely,
E. Cabell Brand

Appendix 3

Suggested Volunteer National and Local Organizations

Each of the following has a "find you local organization feature" at the following web sites:

- The United Way International: http://uwint.org/devfinal
- The American Red Cross: http://www.redcross.org
- The Community Action Partnership: http://www.communityactionpartnership.com
- America's Second Harvest Network: http://www.secondharvest.org
- Chamber of Commerce: http://www.chamberofcommerce.com
- Boy Scouts of America: http://www.scouting.org
- Girl Scouts of the USA: http://www.girlscouts.org
- Rotary International: http://www.rotary.org
- Kiwanis International: http://www.kiwanis.org
- Lions Clubs International: http://www.lionsclubs.org
- The Association of Junior Leagues, Inc. http://www.ajli.org

Or you can do a Google search for any of the following key words:

- Community Service
- Volunteer Organizations
- Service Clubs

Be sure to include the name of your city, town, or ZIP in the search bar to narrow the search to your area. There are thousands of non-profits doing wonderful work in your area that desperately need your skills, help and support.

Appendix 4

GENERAL INFORMATION

Chairman - Cabell Brand Center for International Poverty & Resource Studies

Web Site: www.CabellBrandCenter.org or www.IfNotMeThenWho.org
He is married to the former Shirley Hurt and together they have five children and 13 grandchildren.

For More Information on the author you can also visit the Roanoke Times April 19, 2009 article published on the front page a 4-page article with interactive web videos, video time-line, and 360-degree video panorama on my activities and on the book. This is the latest in cutting-edge interactive news journalism.

Article: http://www.roanoke.com/news/roanoke/wb/200174
Videos: http://www.roanoke.com/wb/xp-202173
Pictures: http://www.roanoke.com/wb/xp-202171
Time Line: http://www.roanoke.com/wb/xp-197307
Panorama: http://www.roanoke.com/wb/xp-199651

You may be interested in accessing the Shepherd Poverty Program at:

Shepherd Poverty Program: http://www.wlu.edu/x12034.xml
11 School Shepherd Poverty Consortium: http://www.wlu.edu/x12109.xml

You can access TAP and CHIP's web page at the addresses below to learn more about their many programs. Please note there is a (S) CHIP program in every state in the country.

TAP: http://www.tapintohope.org/
Roanoke CHIP: http://www.chipofroanokevalley.org/

Breinigsville, PA USA
30 September 2010
246467BV00001B/2/P